ALL KINDS OF MUSICK

All kinds of Musick

THE FIRST 40 YEARS
OF THE
RICHMOND CONCERT SOCIETY

Howard Greenwood

To dear Eleanor
with love
Howard

Jan 2003.

ASHWATER
PRESS

First published in May 2002

Designed and published for Howard Greenwood by
Ashwater Press
68 Tranmere Road
Whitton, Twickenham, Middlesex, TW2 7JB

Printed and bound by
Antony Rowe Ltd, Chippenham, Wiltshire

ISBN 0 9538840 1 5

Foreword

I discovered the Richmond Concert Society some thirty odd years ago, and I use that verb "discovered" quite deliberately: it was like finding hidden treasure. Wonderful chamber music by fine musicians right on my doorstep and for a ridiculously low cost. At that time my job involved extensive travel and for several years I was lucky if I managed to attend just three or four concerts each season, but no worry, there was always at least one event that was worth the whole of the annual subscription. So, for a non-performing listener, a glimpse of the divine through music; for a hard-nosed accountant, value for money; and something special—there was, and is, an extra quality about an RCS evening: a meeting of friends. And even to an obscure ordinary member it was all too obvious that there was a genius behind all this, a young chap called Howard Greenwood.

When I retired from full-time business, I was able to devote more time to the society; and, much to my surprise, ten years ago found myself as chairman! Now I can report as an insider that the Richmond Concert Society is at the forefront of music groups in this country. Nobody can excel us for the range of programmes, the quality of performers, the strength of our finances, and that something extra—the society of friends. There is a strong and active committee working hard with a dedication to maintaining the strength and success of the society, under the continuing wisdom and insight of our director of music, the same Howard Greenwood.

It is fitting that the achievements (and the struggles) of the last forty years should be worthily documented. The story of the Richmond Concert Society is an important part of the cultural life of the borough of Richmond upon Thames, and it is a significant part of the history of music in this country in the 20th century. It has been well written by Howard Greenwood, and it is only fitting that he should be the author, because it is also the story of a life devoted unselfishly to music.

John Ould.

February 2002

Illustrations

Grateful thanks are due to all those who have given permission to reproduce photographs in this book. Where appropriate every effort has been made to trace the copyright holders of other illustrations but without success.

page 22—author; *also* page 39—musicians and author: **photographs by Lady Panufnik**
page 26—Oda Slobodskaya
page 29—Janet Baker
page 32—Raimund Herincx
page 34—Valerie Tryon
page 44—Richard Gandy
page 54—Shura Cherkassky
page 72—Philip Mercier painting: **courtesy National Portrait Gallery**
page 77—Martino Tirimo
page 80—John Ould, Colin Squire and author; *also* page 105—John Ould; *also* page 116—Ian Hobson; *also* page 138—audience at a concert: **photographs by Frances Neale**
page 82—Sidney Harrison
page 84—25th anniversary concert: **courtesy Richmond and Twickenham Times**
page 85—Muriel Dawson
page 90—Imogen Cooper
page 104—Lady Panufnik; *also* page 126—Vellinger Quartet; *also* page 131—Nash Ensemble: **photographs by Keith Saunders**
page 109—Gaudier Ensemble
page 112—CD insert with Anthony Goldstone and Caroline Clemmow
page 117—Maggini String Quartet: **photograph by Gary Childs**
page 127—Joan Rodgers
page 132—Gould Piano Trio: **photograph by Richard Heeps**
page 133—Wihan String Quartet
page 134—Kay Williams: **photograph by Monica Greenwood**
page 135—Stanley Grundy
page 136—Kungsbacka Piano Trio: **photograph by John Batten**

A remembrance of times past
by Raimund Herincx

Howard and I first came to know each other nearly forty years ago. We teamed up in April 1964 to give a recital for the Richmond Concert Society after it had been going for a couple of years. Then in June 1967 we performed Mussorgsky's great song cycle *Songs and Dances of Death* at Richmond Theatre for the Richmond Arts Festival. The rehearsals took place at Howard and Monica's (Mon's) house where I experienced their hospitality, repeated many times over the years and always enjoyed.

Following this, my wife Astra Blair and I were invited by Howard to give a recital which consisted mainly of Brahms—the rarely heard alto-baritone duets and the very attractive Volklieder. I still perform and teach from the copies that Howard gave to us.

Other events followed, but outstanding in my memory was an Arts Council of Wales recital tour of Bala, Harlech, Llandrindod Wells, Llanddewi, Caerphilly, Brecon and other venues during a very severe winter in the 1960s. The repertoire on this tour was enormous and the concerts most successful in wonderful venues, except for the village hall in Llanddewi where a snow-storm and plummeting temperatures forced us to perform in overcoats and gloves, with a piano severely out of tune.

So much musical co-operation and more than forty years of friendship have resulted from the founding of the Richmond Concert Society that I feel especially privileged to write this short note. Howard has never been lost for musical ideas and my great love of lieder has been due to his encouragement and our early performances of Schumann's *Liederkreis*.

My best wishes to the Richmond Concert Society and my very sincere congratulations to Howard after forty years of highly successful concertizing.

Raimund Herincx.

April 2002

> *"The sound of the cornet, flute, harp, sackbut, psaltery, dulcimer, and all kinds of musick."*
>
> The Book of Daniel

Contents

Introduction

The idea of writing the story of the Richmond Concert Society as it approached its 40th season came from my wife, Monica, and the chairman of the Society, John Ould.

The only reason I was entrusted with the task was simply because I was the only one who was there more or less from the start. I set out on the venture with some trepidation, which, so a dictionary informs me, is a state of alarm, anxiety or excitement, which I suppose more or less summed up what I felt.

How should one tell the story of a society whose function is simply to put on concerts? One way would be to itemize each of the concerts which have been presented but I felt that this would border on the tedious as, since we started, well over three hundred concerts have been given. I decided to pick on a few concerts which had a human interest content.

Promoting concerts involves people. At the summit stands the performing musician, but there are many who in their own way contribute to making sure that the whole evening passes smoothly—for example, by stapling programmes together, providing refreshments for the performers, or providing wine for members. Although many things go towards making sure the evening is a success, there still remain the dramas that have occurred, the personality clashes, the fits of temperament and the events not going to plan. They too are all part of the excitement of putting on concerts!

Very early on I found it was difficult to write about what made the society what it is today without explaining the twists and turns of my own life. I hope that this indulgence will be forgiven. The forty years' life of the society coincided with momentous years in the history of this country and I have tried to relate how these political events impacted on the society.

At various stages during the writing of this book I have sought the advice and guidance of friends who are all closely involved with the RCS. At a very early stage John Ould had a look at the first few chapters, and later, when it was largely completed, Peter King, the honorary secretary of the society, spent a considerable time reading what I had written and making very constructive comments. Above all Monica has read, criticised and encouraged me and I am grateful to them all for the help and support they have given.

There comes a time when it is necessary to pass the manuscript (or these days the floppy disks) to the publisher. I have been very fortunate as my publisher Ken Coton, around the corner at Ashwater Press, has shown amazing patience with me and has made many constructive comments. I never realised what an important role a publisher plays in getting a book into a state that it can be printed. Ken was everything I could desire in a publisher and I will always remain grateful to him.

But my last words must be to the members of this great society. They have supported what we set out to achieve all those years ago and have shown a high level of loyalty for which I am most grateful.

Howard Greenwood, Twickenham, March 2002

TO MONICA

This book would never have seen the light of day without the encouragement and support I have always received from my dear wife, Mon. Indeed, as will be seen from the pages of this book, without Mon it is more than likely I would not have been involved with the Richmond Concert Society in the first place.

She has done much more than badger me. She has been through every page and removed many exclamation marks and inserted commas as required. It is in the spirit of love and thanks that I dedicate this modest book to her.

Chapter One

A GLIMPSE INTO THE PAST

It is difficult to accept that the Richmond Concert Society has been in existence for forty years. It seems only yesterday that some of the earlier concerts took place, but the records that still exist at least help piece together the steps that were taken all those years ago to create the society.

The idea of writing the story of the Richmond Concert Society came from my dear wife, Monica. She has been so much a part of the society from its earliest days, and although never a member of the executive she has always been supportive of what we have tried to achieve, and has lived through the many dramas over the years.

The faded press cuttings and the rather tatty brochures dating back to the 1960s were collected into scrapbooks by three dedicated secretaries of the society—Mary Cadman, Denise Latimer-Sayer, and in more recent years Peter King. Without these cuttings, and the minutes of the committee meetings which took place years ago but whose colour has changed from white to yellow with age, it would have been difficult to tell this story, for memory sometimes plays tricks, as I have found much to my surprise.

The story of how the society emerged to its present position contains all the ingredients of a good yarn. There has been drama, as things have not always gone as expected; there have been moments of hilarity and despair; and there have been concerts tinged with tragedy. Many of these emotions were kept from eager audiences assembled to hear great music performed by first-rate artists. I suppose we all love to know what happens backstage, so now the background of some of these concerts can be told for the first time.

Before embarking on the way that the Richmond Concert Society developed, I would like to set the scene of what occurred in the Richmond and Twickenham areas in the past, in other words our musical heritage.

The borough of Richmond upon Thames has had for a long time a tradition of music-making. This involvement in music has taken various forms, such as choirs, as well as concert-promoting organisations. Take, as an example of choral excellence, the Twickenham Choral Society, which was created in October 1921. Each season it continues to go from strength to strength, and the quality of its work is extremely high. In the period 1921 to 1939 the Twickenham Musical Society, for this was the name it was originally known by, was mainly an orchestral society with the choir taking second place. The society started out in close association with Kneller Hall and its first conductor was Lt Col Atkins, who continued until war broke out. There have been over the years a number of conductors and I particularly recall Braden Hunwick, who was a most sensitive interpreter of the choral music of Edward Elgar. Under his baton, I remember hearing an inspired performance of *The Apostles* in 1959, given, if I remember correctly, at All Hallows church, on the Chertsey Road. In 1961 the vicar of that particular church decided to refuse the choir use of the church because he felt that those who came to hear the choir behaved more like a concert audience than a congregation at divine service—how times have changed! Under the baton of Christopher Herrick, its conductor in more recent years, the Twickenham Choral Society has become one of the best choral societies in the whole of west London, and an organisation of which we should all be proud.

The Royal Military School of Music at Kneller Hall has for many years done great work in training musicians and has put Whitton on the musical map. Its weekly concerts during the summer months are enjoyed by large audiences, who also clearly enjoy the fireworks which accompany the music. Recently it has encouraged our young musicians from the borough's schools to join forces with its own musicians, and what a wonderful experience this has been. Other choirs, such as the Barnes Choir and the Hampton Choral Society, continue upholding the choral tradition which is so much part of this country's heritage.

But it is not just choral societies which have flourished. Between the wars there existed a concert society, similar in many ways to the Richmond Concert Society, which brought to Twickenham many of the outstanding musicians of the day, such as Myra Hess and Solomon. I remember a few years ago meeting the last remaining member of the committee and discussing with her many of the fine musicians who played before the Second World War in Twickenham. She had lovingly kept all the old programmes in a scrapbook, and it made fascinating reading.

Going far back in history there existed an organisation known as the Richmond Musical Society which was reported in the first edition of Richmond Notes. This publication described itself as a monthly record of local information. Dated March 1863 and predating what is now known as the Richmond and Twickenham Times by ten years, Richmond Notes set out to provide a "periodical publication devoted to the diffusion of information of a local nature, and having local interests as its principal subject". It devoted quite a lot of space in its first issue to the Richmond Musical Society. It appears that this organisation consisted mainly of amateur music-makers set up "to enable them to practise that class of music, and attain that precision of execution, which the cultivated taste of the present day demands". All very worthy but the objective was not always attained. The report continues: "To say that the Richmond Musical Society has attained perfection would be absurd, but its members exhibit, at least in instrumental music, a degree of skill which is more than respectable, and verges at times upon the excellent. Of its vocal qualifications we cannot say as much. Ladies who are not professional object to exhibit their talent in public, and the male voices, we fear, do not study sufficiently, or practise often enough together, to fulfil the objects of the composer." Oh dear—critics never change. The concert reported upon was apparently only the third they had given, and how long the Richmond Musical Society lasted is not known. The concert was given in the great room of the Castle Hotel. This somewhat condescending review of the concert appeared alongside a report announcing the approaching marriage of the Prince of Wales to Alexandra, described as the Fair Maid of Denmark. This was a strange and pompous reporting of the engagement, as it reminded its readers that "It is now two centuries and a half since a "Royal Dane" graced the throne of England, and it is with no small pleasure that we hail now a return to the alliance of that northern race with our own."

During the Second World War concerts continued to be given in London and the best known were the National Gallery lunchtime concerts. Run by Myra Hess, these concerts gave so much comfort to war-weary Londoners. Outside London an organisation known as CEMA (Committee for the Encouragement of Music and the Arts) was created, and this body enlisted the talents of outstanding musicians, who travelled all over the country giving recitals. The objectives of CEMA, apart from giving work to musicians and actors, included the keeping up of morale during the war years. By the closing stages of the war CEMA had been responsible for just over 6,000 concerts. I remember these concerts in my home town of Shrewsbury in Shropshire, which included recitals by artists of the calibre of Clifford Curzon playing Schubert and Oda Slobodskaya, the distinguished Russian soprano, singing Mussorgsky. Little did I realise how involved I was going to become with her some years later. With the end of the war, under the inspiration of John Maynard Keynes, one of the Bloomsbury set, the Arts Council of Great Britain was created, and to fill a gap in our cultural life music societies started springing up all over the place. The Richmond area was no exception. The main concert-giving society for some time, before the setting up of the Richmond Concert Society, was the Barnes Music Club. I remember with great affection Myrtle Lane, who ran it so efficiently and with so much dedication. The secretary was Connie Hewlett, who seemed to have the ability to upset not only her own committee but other committees as well. The club made the mistake—which eventually cost them dearly—of setting up a choir as part of the music club. Such an arrangement never seems to work satisfactorily, as there are two sides of the same family making claims on what money is available. It certainly did not work in the case of the Barnes Music Club as petty jealousies split the activities of this fine organisation. The Barnes Choir has continued and has won many accolades during the years, and the Barnes Music Club has also continued, although on a more modest scale than at its height in the 1960s.

Another interesting music society that existed in Richmond was based at Norfolk Lodge on Richmond Hill. This was known as the New Atlantis and was an offshoot of what seemed to be a theosophy sect. It was very small and run by a set of delightful people such as David Shillan, who was to become one of the first chairmen of the newly formed Richmond upon Thames Arts Council. The concerts attracted, if I remember rightly, about twenty people and they had the lovely idea of not charging for the wine they always served in the interval, because this had been paid for by those who had come to the previous concert. When introducing the concert, the chairman would ask with great grace that those present show their appreciation by making a reasonable donation so that those coming to the next event would be able to enjoy a glass of wine. The interval refreshment idea, now such a feature of the Richmond Concert Society, could well be traced back to this example set by the New Atlantis. I recall hearing at Norfolk Lodge in the 1960s a pianist by the name of Bernard Roberts, who played many times for them, as he has for us, and the late lamented Celia Arieli, a pianist of great sensitivity, as well as Maria Donska.

In Hampton there was also activity around the late 1950s, when the composer Mátyás Seiber started the Hampton and Teddington Music Society. Although very small it had its own loyal following and, no doubt because of Seiber's influence, the emphasis was on the contemporary music scene. Mátyás Seiber was a composer of originality whose music is sadly neglected today. Although he always regarded himself as an English composer, he was in fact born in Hungary and studied under Zoltan Kodály. Arriving in England in 1935 he became a tutor at Morley College. Seiber was influenced in his compositions by Bartok and Schoenberg. The Hampton club carried on for a few years after Mátyás Seiber died in a tragic road accident in South Africa, following which it gradually faded away.

One concert which the club presented I recall with great pleasure, even after all these years. It took place in early March 1962 and played to a miserably small audience. The venue was the large hall in York House, which has been renamed in more recent times the Clarendon Hall, and the four artists who performed were Dorothy Dorrow, an attractive soprano who must have possessed perfect pitch because her ability to sing what she did was quite amazing; William Bennett, who was the flautist; and two pianists—Richard Rodney Bennett and Susan Bradshaw. The programme was exciting but suicidal. It included some songs by Messiaen, early pieces but quite enchanting; music by Webern; and a piece by Boulez, who at that period was regarded as an *enfant terrible*. Not a programme to have the public banging on the doors to gain admittance, but satisfying all the same.

In the Kingston area Michael Dobson, who played the oboe with some distinction, formed the Thames Concert Society which gave concerts of baroque music, using a small orchestra based in the parish church.

Exciting times, and one cannot help but feel that we are much less adventurous in the way programmes are designed these days. It seems that nowadays the formula it is necessary to adopt is to insert a challenging new work between established, well known and loved repertoire. There is nothing intrinsically wrong in this approach—it is just a way one can attract an audience and allow them a chance to know what new music is being written.

There is one other concert society that I need to mention. It was called the Richmond Concerts Society and, I hasten to add, had no connection whatsoever with The Richmond Concert Society, the subject of this story. How many concerts it organised is not known despite searching the pages of local newspapers around the time. It was presented by kind invitation of Dr and Mrs Swann and their son Donald Swann. I recall "Bunny" Swann, as she was known, and her very close involvement with the Barnes Music Club in the 1950s and early 1960s. Donald Swann became very well known as half of the highly successful Flanders and Swann team. He was a witty and talented composer and although the passage of time has dimmed his contribution to light music, his song *Mud, Mud, Glorious Mud* became part of 20th century cabaret material. His collaboration with Michael Flanders started in 1956 and continued for many years. It was in 1951 that he extended an invitation to members of the Richmond Concerts Society to come and hear Gerard Hoffnung. At that time Donald was unknown, as his teaming up with Flanders was still five years away. The members of the society were invited to the Richmond community centre on Sunday 16th March 1951 at 7.30pm to come and hear Hoffnung give an informal talk on Ravel's opera *L'Enfant et les Sortilèges*. I found this information very interesting when it surfaced some years ago; whilst chairman at that time of the Richmond upon Thames Arts Council, I brought to the Orleans Gallery in Twickenham an exhibition of the cartoons and drawings of Gerard Hoffnung, which turned out to be a great success and had to be repeated several times by public request.

Apparently one of the reasons for inviting Hoffnung to Richmond was to draw attention to a forthcoming performance of the Ravel opera, to be given by members of the Chanticleer Marionettes at the Richmond community centre. The centre will reappear again in forthcoming chapters. It has, I am delighted to say, disappeared from view, having been pulled down a number of years ago to make way for a Waitrose supermarket, which is certainly caring for Richmond much more than the community centre ever did. I can only hope that Dr and Mrs Swann did not run into the ghastly things that happened to us when we had really no option but to use this particular venue in the early days of our society.

Very little else is known about that particular society; the beginnings of our Richmond Concert Society are similarly shrouded in some mystery. On a May evening in 1961 five ladies and three gentlemen met "to discuss the organising of a series of concerts to be held in Richmond". Although there was a rapid movement of personnel in the first few months of the society, what is known for certain is that this May meeting was held at number 1 St Helena Terrace in Richmond. Present were Mrs Williams, Miss Dunn, Mrs Griffiths, Mrs McDonald, Mrs Grist, Mr Kileen, Mr Todd and Mr Houston. I would like to say that this group had the highest intentions of starting a concert society in Richmond, with the main objective being the welfare of the old and the infirm who loved music but due to their age or infirmity could no longer travel to the London concert halls. I would like to have said that, but the facts tell a quite different story, although I am sure that such an objective might have been in the minds of some of those who attended the first meeting.

According to Jill Grist, the whole thing came into being because these formidable ladies clearly wanted to make their mark on Richmond and the whole idea of starting a concert society was ridiculed by their nearest and dearest! Jill was so determined that this is how it all started that I have to believe her. The driving force was Decia Griffiths, who was an amateur mezzo-soprano with a reasonable voice, and she was certainly ambitious to show it off. This was, I believe, the prime reason for her initial involvement. Miss Dunn also saw a possible outlet for her cello playing, as indeed did Mr Todd for his piano playing. At that first meeting they decided on what they would call the group and they fixed on Richmond Concert Club, but this name only lasted until the next meeting when the name Richmond Concert Society was adopted. By November 1961 the first committee was agreed; members of this formative committee were Diana Dyer, Louise Buchner, Patricia Hobbs, Mrs Williams, Decia Griffiths, Mrs McDonald, Mrs Young, Joan Caplan, Jill Grist, Malcolm Gray and Edward Johnston. Of this committee Decia Griffiths took over the role of chairman, Jill Grist was appointed as secretary, and Patricia Hobbs became membership secretary, although at this early stage with no members she really had very little to do! Edward Johnston took on the critical position of treasurer, although he volunteered to act also as organising secretary. Edward, who was a senior civil servant and worked hard helping to set up this fledgeling organisation, later severed his relationship with the RCS. He was knighted for his work as a government actuary.

How does one set about starting a new concert society at a time when the Barnes Music Club is so strong and influential? The decision was taken to put on three pilot concerts to test if there was an interest among the people of Richmond. At that early stage it was very Richmond based, and was run on a very amateurish basis, a point that was to create problems quite soon in the history of this new and struggling society.

The first thing that needed to be settled was the constitution, or the rules that were to apply. Help was forthcoming from the National Federation of Music Societies, who provided a draft constitution. The management of the society was vested in the chairman, an honorary secretary, an honorary treasurer and a committee of not less than four, and not more than seven. The society had the right to receive donations, grants in aid or financial guarantees—the founding fathers possibly had no idea how necessary this provision was going to prove, as much later the society started to attract sponsorship from a number of companies and individuals. It was also laid down that whilst membership was by payment of a subscription, nevertheless "single tickets may be issued to the public, to any or all of its concerts as may be desirable."

The income or property of the society "wheresoever derived shall be applied solely towards the promotion of the objects of the society as set forth in the rules, and no portion thereof shall be paid or transferred directly or indirectly by way of dividend, bonus, or by payment of a professional fee to any member or members of the society appearing as artists at its concerts." This rule is written in concrete and although professional artists who are members have performed for the society, or have given professional advice on a number of subjects over the years, no fee has ever been paid. Before they set about writing a constitution very modest fees of £7 were in fact paid to performers who were also members of the organising committee.

As the needs of the society have changed over the years, it has been necessary to make certain adjustments to the original constitution, but much of what was laid down in the early 1960s still applies. Certain changes that have been made reflect the stringent rules that have been imposed in recent years by the charity commissioners. Such changes have all been made with the consent of the members, generally by a show of hands at a concert.

So, with the governing rules in place, the next step was to set about organising the three concerts. Although the creation of a new society was welcomed by the Richmond and Twickenham Times, the paper had to admit that the new society was only able to attract "a moderately good audience", which, bearing in mind that the Parkshot Rooms seated only about sixty people, meant that only about twenty or so actually attended this inaugural concert. It was held on the 19th October 1961 and the three artists were Pauline Dunn, a cellist, John Douglas Todd, a pianist, and the chairman of the RCS, Decia Griffiths. The programme was an attractive one, and started with Decia singing a group of songs by Purcell followed by a performance of the Richard Strauss cello sonata. This by all accounts was not a satisfactory performance as the pianist, clearly not a very seasoned or experienced performer, effectively blotted out the sound of the cello. John Douglas Todd was more effective when he had only himself to consider, and his performance of the third piano sonata of Prokofiev was generally considered coherent. The impression one gleans is that he had a technique to cope with the technical demands of Prokofiev and Chopin, but little else. A group of folksongs from Decia and some cello solos completed the programme.

A month later another pilot concert took place. The singer was the young Canadian soprano Annon Lee Silver, who sang Berlioz's *Nuits d'Été* and a group of Hugo Wolf's Goethe lieder. This exceptionally talented and attractive young singer certainly won the attention of the newspaper critic, who forecast that she would have a good career. Unfortunately, her full potential was never realised as, after singing for a season at Glyndebourne, she died of cancer at the age of thirty—a great loss to music. The violinist that evening was 17-year-old Garcia Asenio who bravely played Beethoven's *Kreutzer* sonata. It was, so it seems, not a convincing performance.

In March 1962 the third of the pilot concerts took place and this was hailed by the Richmond and Twickenham Times as "the best evening yet". It was given by Carl Pini, Colin Tilney and Dennis Nesbitt, performing a range of music from Handel to modern works. What was interesting about this concert was the inclusion of *Two Inventions* by Stephen Dodgson, a composer whose works have frequently appeared in our programmes over the past forty years. Stephen has acknowledged the fact that the RCS were responsible to

Handbill for the third pilot concert.

RICHMOND CONCERT SOCIETY

presents

CARL PINI - violin

COLIN TILNEY - harpsichord

DENNIS NESBITT - viola da gamba

AT THE

PARKSHOT ROOMS

ON

WEDNESDAY, MARCH 7th, at 8 p.m.

In a Programme of works by
SCARLATTI · BACH · HANDEL · RAMEAU · CABEZÓN
YSAŸE and OTHERS

TICKETS 6/-

Obtainable from Philharmonic Records Ltd., 5-6 Paved Court, Richmond, and at the door

REFRESHMENTS AVAILABLE

a marked degree for the piano sonatas he has composed, one of which received its first performance at an RCS concert. This third pilot concert was my first contact with the Richmond Concert Society and I was intrigued by what they were trying to do. At this stage I think I must call on the memories of my wife Monica, who took a pivotal role in what was to come:

"It must have been early in the New Year of 1962 that having a couple of hours to myself, as my daughter Julia was at a playgroup, I wandered into the underwear department of Marks & Spencer in Richmond and noticed another woman of about my age eyeing me. There seemed something very familiar about her. We both cautiously approached each other and were amused to find that the intervening fifteen years had changed us little. Decia (née Robinson) was my respected deputy head girl at the Blackpool Grammar School where during wartime I had been evacuated because my father's ministry had moved there from Whitehall. Post war we had returned to London and subsequently I had met and married Howard, a Shropshire lad, a gifted and prize-winning pianist, who had trained at the Guildhall School of Music and Drama. In the meantime Decia had married the Labour MP for Manchester Exchange, Will Griffiths, and settled happily in Richmond. Decia had recently discovered the joys of amateur singing and started having singing lessons at the Guildhall School of Music and Drama.

"With the responsibilities of marriage Howard had decided to launch on a daytime career as an underwriter in the City of London, but immersed himself in music in his own free time, occasionally doing some teaching and performing to supplement the family income. Soon after this chance meeting I invited Decia to our home and she arrived clutching her music, to be coached by Howard at the piano to perform again for the new organisation that she and a few other community-minded women had decided to form in Richmond. After numerous committee meetings and a couple of inaugural concerts in the latter part of 1961, the Richmond Concert Society put on one more concert in March 1962 when Carl Pini and two others performed. From that time onward Howard became involved as music director for the first season of concerts to start in the autumn of 1962."

So we were on our way. We had a very small core audience, no money but plenty of commitment. Could we succeed? Little did I realise then the extent to which I would soon fall out with a number of my colleagues on the committee. I even offered to resign as music director, but the reasons for this should become clearer as we look at our first decade of concerts.

Chapter Two

ON THE MOVE IN THE SWINGING SIXTIES

After the March 1962 concert by Carl Pini and his friends, we were all ready to plan our first season. One problem that we had, and one that persisted for some years, was a lack of money. So it was decided that we would hold a fund-raising concert to see if we could put a few pounds into the kitty. This concert took place on the 28th July, and like many of our early events was held in one of the Maids of Honour houses, which so elegantly grace Richmond Green. On this occasion it was number 2, which at that time was lived in by Dr and Mrs Barlow, and from what I remember of the concert after all these years it was a success. Decia Griffiths sang again—this time some Bach—and it was one of the few occasions when I sat down and played a harpsichord. Jeremy Barlow, the son of the house, played the flute. Later Jeremy was to make a major contribution to music-making in this country in the baroque field.

The star of the evening was the soprano Helga Mott who sang some lieder by Mendelssohn, Schubert and Richard Strauss. Helga, who lived around the corner in one of the Wardrobe houses belonging to the old Richmond Palace, was to do several master-classes in lieder for the society in seasons to come, with a great deal of success. This concert raised the sum of £27. Maybe not much in today's values but in 1962 it gave us much needed funds to contemplate a full season of concerts.

So on Tuesday the 2nd October 1962 we opened the first season of concerts. The preliminary concerts had established a small core of loyal followers. There was so much goodwill surrounding this new venture in its early years, and many were generous in giving us much needed support. The venue for our first concert, a piano recital, was the Richmond community centre. It was the only hall in Richmond and not a good one at that; indeed, my memories of this hall border on the hysterical. The pianist on that occasion was Irene Kohler. Irene was, I recall, generous in the level of fee she requested which was just as well because there was very little money available! She had had a most successful career and in that year of 1962 had completed her second world tour. Her active career, in fact, extended until 1980 when she undertook a tour of Poland. In later years I used to meet Irene at parties given by a mutual friend, Sidney Harrison. She never missed an opportunity of seeking another engagement. Irene, at the opening concert, started with Busoni's great transcription of Bach's organ toccata in C major and also played the opus 109 sonata of Beethoven, the Lennox Berkeley piano sonata and a group of Chopin. Irene was married to a delightful man, Dr Harry Waters, a medical practitioner in Barnes; she was closely involved with the Barnes Music Club. I recall with warmth the encouragement we received from Myrtle Lane of the Barnes Music Club. She could easily have viewed us as a rival and a threat but so genuine was she and so dedicated to music that she was kindness itself.

This concert—and we date our existence from this time—was the first occasion I had a go at writing programme notes. They were very modest and the whole programme and notes scarcely filled a page of A4 paper folded into half. Over the years I have written thousands of programme notes and in them I have tried to write for a very special audience, the members of the RCS. My intention is to give as much help as I can to explain a particular work in two ways, firstly by giving some background information about the composer, and then by mentioning some tags for the listener to take hold of in order, hopefully, to increase enjoyment of the piece.

We tried in that first season to give value for money, and this desire has continued over the past forty years. The subscription covering all the events was one guinea. By this stage the committee consisted of Decia as chairman, Edward Johnston as organising secretary and treasurer, Brigit Barlow, Joan Caplan, Diana Dyer, Malcolm Gray, Jill Grist,

The author—forty years ago!

Patricia Hobbs and Diana Young. From the start I have acted as director of music.

To save on fees, I was involved in the second concert on the 6th November when Richard Gandy, generally known as Dick, who was a member of our very small society, gave a lieder recital. This consisted of those great Schubert songs to poems by Heine, which sit almost like a sub song cycle within the overall *Schwanengesang* cycle. Then followed Britten's *Winter Words* cycle—over the years we were to perform all the major Britten song cycles at various recitals. We concluded the recital with Schumann's *Dichterliebe*—one of many performances of this impressive cycle that I gave with Dick and a number of other singers over the years. We used the drawing room of 36 Sheen Road, a delightful Georgian house which was kindly loaned to us that evening by Dr and Mrs Melville Mackenzie. The critic of the Richmond and Twickenham Times, who was also the editor, R V Ward, raved about Dick's voice, which if I recall correctly was in good shape that evening.

A violin recital by Yfrah Neaman, partnered by Paul Hamburger, was given in January, again at the community centre in Richmond. To give you some idea of the problems this hall presented to us, and I am sure to many other organisations as well, I need only quote from the review that appeared in the Richmond and Twickenham Times about this recital: "It had not occurred to the administrators of this municipal palace of culture that the continual bangs and bumps overhead might cause some slight distraction to these two fine musicians and the people who had come to hear them." Richmond has never addressed the need for a proper hall either in Richmond or the borough at large.

Fortunately neither Neaman nor Hamburger got a fit of temperament about the awful noises they had to battle against. The main works they played were a sonata by Prokofiev, the one in F minor, and Brahms' D minor violin sonata.

We also went to the home of Isador and Joan Caplan at 144 Richmond Hill, which later was acquired by the Richmond Hill Hotel when Isador and Joan moved down into Petersham. This was for a talk by Harold Rosenthal entitled The Life of an Opera Critic. He was the editor of the magazine Opera, and this was the first of a number of talks that were included in our early seasons.

We continued that first season of eight events with a string quartet concert. Now, looking back after all these years, I recall the agonies that the committee went through before they agreed with my suggestion that we should invite a well known string quartet to come to Richmond. Was there an audience for this type of music? I argued that if there wasn't, it was up to us to make one, and we needed a quartet to have a balanced programme. Eventually after much argument they agreed and Carl Pini, who had now been made a patron of the society, came with the London String Quartet and played Haydn, Beethoven and Shostakovich.

Two more events took place and of the eight shown in the brochure, five were for members only and not available to the public. These member concerts were the ones held in private houses, and in April 1963 we had a talk by James Gilbert, who had written the musical *Grab Me a Gondola*, and he chatted away to members about working for the theatre and television. This was held at number 2 Maids of Honour Row, Richmond Green. "Biddy" Barlow, now on the committee, was so generous to us in those early days in the way she allowed members to enjoy what we were able to offer, in the comfort of her large drawing room. These visits to fine Richmond houses were always appreciated and proved to be a major attraction.

The season finished with a summer serenade concert in the garden of Harrington Lodge in Petersham. This concert was conducted, I believe, by Nicholas Conran who later was to be the conductor of Gemini Opera, whose performances of grand opera at Richmond Theatre delighted audiences for many years.

So we had got through our first critical season. Would we be able to continue? Whilst music lovers in Richmond were prepared to pay their one guinea to belong, they tended not to come to the events. We had to prove ourselves and this took time.

When we started planning the second season—1963-64—we were gaining in confidence as to where we wanted to get to but, as always, we were fighting for an audience. Many of the concerts played to a small number of dedicated followers and I recall, with a great deal of affection, an elderly lady who came to every concert and who always wore red wellington boots. I cannot recall her name, but at the time we called her Miss Red Boots. After so many years I can still see her in my mind's eye. The fact that she made the effort to turn out in all weathers gave us all the encouragement we badly needed.

The committee was still reluctant to have a string quartet in the season's programme. This irritated me but I had to think up an alternative evening. One persistent committee member suggested an evening of Indian music, and whilst I suspect a number of members went into a trance hearing one raga after another (and each raga seemed to last for ages), at least it was a change. I decided at that moment that I would fight my corner with a greater determination for a string quartet the following year.

Actually the season got off to a fine start when an outstanding pianist of the day, Denis Matthews, gave a recital in the dreaded community centre. Playing some Bach preludes and fugues, a group of Mozart, a selection of Chopin preludes and Bartok's Bulgarian dances, Denis displayed a fine technique and what is more an innate musical understanding, which is needed to bring off Schumann's *Scenes from Childhood*. It was a brave move to engage such a well known pianist so early in our existence, but we hit a major obstacle early on. Denis would only play on a full sized Steinway and nothing else. Hiring pianos is expensive at the best of times, but at that time Steinway's led the field in expensive hire. It was also at a time when Steinway's employed a man who was really very difficult to deal with. The damage this one man did to Steinway's business was considerable, before he was eventually removed. Our problem was solved when Denis agreed to pay the extra costs involved in hiring the Steinway—so we went ahead.

He was happy and so were we, and for the first time, with such a celebrity to start the season, we had a full house. It sounds good saying this but really the Richmond community centre was quite small and I would guess that the audience possibly numbered a hundred. As the critic rightly commented, the tone of the Steinway was really not right for a hall with a superabundance of bass response.

I could write a volume about the next concert. It aged both Monica and myself—and in 1963 we were quite young! It came about in this way. Some years after I finished my training at the Guildhall School of Music and Drama, I received an exploratory letter from them to see if there was any future in forming an old students' reunion club, and to launch it they gave a modest reception and a small concert. One of the professors who gave her services and sang on that evening was the legendary Russian singer, Oda Slobodskaya. She sang Mussorgsky's *Nursery Songs*. It was sheer magic and I plucked up all the courage I could and asked her if she would sing for the Richmond Concert Society. She agreed in principle and from that moment our problems started.

I had heard her during the war years in my home town of Shrewsbury, when she gave a CEMA concert, and was bowled over by her personality and voice. I agreed on a fee and we were able to make the concert a members-only one and used for the first and only time the octagonal music room of Asgill House, on the riverside at Richmond. This in itself was a selling point, as nobody had seen the inside of this well known house for years, and soon all the available seats were taken. For weeks before the concert Oda pestered both Monica and myself over this detail and that, and a day before the concert she informed us that she did not want her money in the form of a cheque but in cash only. She also made it quite clear that she did not want any hospitality and that she would leave straight after the concert, as she had friends in Kew who were going to look after her. This was fine

Oda Slobodskaya, a legend who came and sang (and talked) during the early days of the society.

for us as we had nothing along these lines organised. What we did not know was that the two delightful elderly men who loaned us their house had decided to engage caterers for a post concert reception.

Oda arrived and her first demand was for me to get on my knees and with a buttonhook manipulate the buttons on her leather shoes. That done she went in and delighted the audience. I failed to get a seat, so stood outside in the hall, but I still have the sound of her voice singing, in Russian, *Black Eyes*. The Richmond and Twickenham Times devoted many columns to her with the heading Singer is a Legend of our Time—and she was. "A combination of acting, elocution, musical interpretation and performance on the most difficult, complex and unpredictable instrument that could possibly be devised." So wrote Reg Ward in his review of this amazing concert. After the concert Oda retired to her dressing-room, and when she came out and saw the dining room table groaning with food and wine she huffed and puffed before being whisked off to have dinner with her friends in Kew.

Next morning she was on the phone and was very angry. "Why," she demanded, "did you not tell me that there was a reception after the concert?" I replied that I had no idea that the owners would be so generous but Oda would not have it. "Did you realise that my friends in Kew gave me a few sandwiches and that was all?" Anyway we parted friends and although she nearly drove me insane, I still look back with great affection on this great singer. We continued our friendship until her sad death some years later, when the poor soul had to have both legs removed after gangrene had set in. So great was the impact she made on her audience during that first concert that she agreed to sing again another season, so I will return to Oda later with fond memories.

Another concert that season which I am proud of was the one we gave in February 1964. It was an ambitious affair, as we mounted a performance of Sir William Walton's *Façade*. When this entertainment was first produced in the 1920s the Edith Sitwell poems appeared to emerge through the mouth of a black cardboard face. I wanted to try and recreate this in the Richmond community centre and achieved it to some extent. It had been tried out some months earlier at the National Physical Laboratory by their music society. The Edith Sitwell poems were recited at our concert by Humphrey Burton, who went on to direct some of the most outstanding opera on television and also wrote definitive biographies of Leonard Bernstein and Yehudi Menuhin. Speaking to Humphrey in more recent times he told me that he has a vivid memory of that event. His late wife, Gretel Davis, also took part. The instrumental ensemble was conducted by a young unknown musician by the name of Roger Norrington. He was thirty years old then and his career still had a few years to develop. Now one of our more distinguished conductors, he was knighted for his great service to music. I was sitting at the back of the hall for this concert and I recall a figure coming in when the lights had dimmed—it was Vladimir Ashkenazy. This was a surprise to me; I assume he was a guest of Roger Norrington.

Another concert that season I particularly remember—well, I could hardly forget it as I was at the piano accompanying one of the leading singers of the day, Raimund Herincx. It was in the community centre and the programme was a most demanding one, not only for Raimund but for myself as, after a performance of a Schumann song cycle, we ended the recital with a group of Hugo Wolf songs. The climax was Wolf's setting of the Goethe poem *Prometheus*. This is like performing a piano concerto with its crashing octaves. It needs a great deal of stamina and concentration and on that evening the Richmond community centre was well up to its usual tricks. As Raimund and I got to the emotional summit of this great piece, a side door of the community centre opened and a rather raucous female voice said "See you next week, Nell," to which Nell replied "Okay, see you next week!" The atmosphere we had tried to build up was destroyed in an instant.

We also had an organ recital by the sub-organist at Westminster Abbey, Simon Preston, who went on to become the organist and master of the choristers at the abbey. He very kindly gave his services so that we could try to build up some reserves, which were fast diminishing.

It was during this season that we introduced the opera scheme whereby we were able to take block bookings for opera at Covent Garden and Sadler's Wells, at a reduced rate. This became very popular and was effectively administered by Patricia Hobbs. This facility continued for a number of years, and was only discontinued when we ran into a financial cash flow problem which left us no alternative but to terminate the scheme, albeit with great regret.

Around May 1964 some degree of strain was apparent within the committee and clearly we were approaching a point where the future of the RCS was in doubt. I had become frustrated by having to use the Richmond community centre and really wanted to seek out better venues, if necessary outside the confines of Richmond town. This was not viewed with any favour by my fellow committee members. Decia Griffiths had tendered her resignation as chairman and I felt that I could not continue as director of music unless matters changed, so I tendered my resignation but, like Decia, agreed to continue on the committee. Edward Johnston also decided that he had had enough as organising secretary, so he resigned as well.

We all believed in what we were doing, of that there was no doubt. The problem was that we saw the future in various ways and it was proving difficult to reconcile our differences. The treasurer at that time, George Tyrer, a delightful man, was also concerned about the financial side, and he started murmuring under his breath that we might well have reached the time when we should call it a day and wind the society up.

I was finding it difficult to work with Edward Johnston as our views on how musicians should be approached differed considerably. This was a true clash of personalities and I was well aware that Edward was well liked by a number of persons whose opinion I respected. His attitude was to give musicians a meal but hardly any fee—a view I regarded as an insult to my fellow musicians, as it almost implied that all musicians were starving in London garrets. But then Edward realised how lacking in funds we were at that time so his attitude was perhaps understandable.

My approach was to give musicians as good a fee as we could possibly manage. I was quite prepared to negotiate keenly on fees, and have continued to do so. I believed passionately in keeping the society going despite the pessimistic vibes I received from other quarters. As it happened I withdrew my resignation and Edward Johnston succeeded Decia as chairman. I was prepared to see how this worked out but in the meantime we had a new season to finalise.

My objections to the Richmond community centre were accepted by my colleagues, and we looked out for new halls to present our concerts. It has always baffled me that a civilised town such as Richmond has no hall suitable for high quality performers. We seem to have concentrated on theatres but not on halls. When the Queen Charlotte Hall was built some years later a golden chance was missed. For the 1964-65 season we had an impressive build-up of artists but then made what was in retrospect an awful mistake. We were aware of a new hall in Church Road which was dedicated to looking after the needs of the old. It was named after a former mayor of Richmond, and the Meadows Hall became our main venue for the 1964-65 season, but it was not really suitable as the ceiling was too low and the sound lacked brightness.

The opening concert was given by the brilliant John Ogdon. This was the first time that John played for the society. His programme was a tough one for any pianist—the second book of Chopin studies, a Mozart sonata, Ravel's *Gaspard de la Nuit*, and to end, one of the most dazzling of all piano works, *Islamey* by Balakirev. I recall that something went wrong with our printing arrangements and no programmes were available. I suggested to John that I introduce each item, but he felt that he would get better contact with the audience if he did the introductions himself. Unfortunately John had a very soft, gentle voice and no one could hear what he was talking about.

The other outstanding recital, also at the Meadows Hall, was a song recital by Janet Baker. I recall going to see her just before the concert started and finding her totally immersed in the score of the songs she was going to perform. I was struck by the sheer

Janet Baker, who gave a memorable recital.

dedication and professionalism of this great singer. She gave a memorable recital, although she was not well served by the dead acoustics of the Meadows Hall.

We also had a concert by the London Soloists Ensemble which was led by Nicholas Roth, who had played in his youth with Bartok. This ensemble, which consisted of four violins, two violas, two cellos, a double bass and harpsichord, made an excellent sound. They played music by Vivaldi, Telemann and Shostakovich. Altogether the 1964-65 season consisted of eight events including three talks, of which one was given at 234 Kew Road by Stephen Dodgson who spoke about Vivaldi and *The Four Seasons*, and one at the home of Helga Mott where we heard Winifred Ferrier talking about her sister Kathleen.

We had pulled out all the stops for the 1964-65 season in order to attract more members but the result was disappointing. As that season started the membership level had fallen to 94, and we were in the red to an unhealthy level of £55. I would not exactly say that panic had taken over but we were nearly at our wits' end. Morale among the committee had dropped to an all-time low. We were nearly at the point of winding the society up.

I put to my colleagues the programme for the 1965-66 season. This included a return of Oda Slobodskaya, despite all the problems she had caused on her previous visit. I called on her at her north London flat, and this had its light side. Oda lived in the same block as the notorious Christine Keeler. The scandal had taken place in 1963 but she still lived there. I needed to enquire where the flats were when I emerged from the Underground and was viewed with much suspicion by the person I asked. Finding my way into the building I walked down the corridor and heard coming from one apartment loud pop music. I checked the number and could not believe that it tallied with Oda's flat. I rang the bell and after some moments the door opened, and standing there was an old woman with long grey hair hanging down her back. She looked like a witch!

Informing me that she had the flu, she kindly asked me in and we talked about the possibility of her doing another concert in Richmond. She agreed and what surprised me even more, she agreed to come at the same fee.

As we had had such an unsatisfactory experience at the Meadows Hall we had no alternative but to go back to the community centre. Oda came with John Wills, a fine accompanist of the day. The idea was that Oda was going to give a song recital along the lines of the one she had given on her first visit. But it seemed that this was not going to be possible. John Wills took me aside and told me that Oda's doctor had said that she had a heart complaint and that she must only sing two songs. Obviously a disappointment but I had to accept it. I had heard her tell her life story in front of an audience and it made an such an enthralling story that I asked her to do the same that evening. She agreed and as usual she enchanted everyone but would not stop singing. She had an audience and, true professional that she was, she wanted to make sure that they had a good evening. I was concerned about her health in view of what John Wills had said, but she survived. We became close friends and I remember Monica's mother, who was also studying with me at the Guildhall School of Music and Drama, telling me that she was once in conversation with Oda and the talk came around to her career and family matters. She had left Russia after the revolution, had sung all over the world and made a great impact at Covent Garden in Tchaikowsky's *Eugene Onegin*, but she confided to my mother-in-law that she would have given it all away to have had children. But it was not to be. A great singer and character and all we have today are some wonderful recordings she made.

That season we also had a piano recital by Malcolm Binns, a fine and, I feel, a neglected pianist, again at the community centre. We also went back to the Parkshot Rooms and put on a song recital there, and continued to use private houses such as number 1 Maids of Honour Row, Richmond Green— the home of Lady Dorothy Meynell, a wonderful lady who came frequently to our concerts and was always so very supportive. At her home Stephen Dodgson and his wife Jane Clark (who had been a fellow student with me at the Guildhall School) gave a piano duet evening. We had talks about opera at Helga Mott's home, and the other main concerts consisted of the Budapest Piano Trio and for the first time a choral concert at St Peter's church in Petersham, a very historic church. This was our first church concert and opened a chink of hope for future concerts in the borough's churches, despite the resistance felt by certain members on the executive committee.

Marianne Duncan served as the secretary of the society during the 1965-66 season and continued carrying out this important role for some seasons to come. She was the wife of a distinguished Queen's Council, Colin Duncan. However, by the time we set out on the 1966-67 season the committee had changed radically. Edward Johnston had resigned as chairman, and Decia Griffiths, who had remained on the committee after leaving the post of chairman, had also decided to leave the committee as indeed had Diana Dyer. In fact, no-one concerned with the pilot concerts was any longer involved. I found myself in the dual role of chairman and music director in an attempt to keep the show on the road, despite the worries that my dear old trusted friend George Tyrer, the treasurer, had about our financial position.

Raimund Herincx, a leading baritone of Covent Garden and English National Opera, who later sang Wotan in Wagner's Ring *all over the world. Raimund was a frequent performer at our concerts in the formative years.*

So here we were trying to put on professional concerts on a shoestring in venues which were less than satisfactory—but back with regret to the community centre we had to go! As I saw it we needed to call on friendly musicians to help us out; I have never forgotten their loyalty and I would like to think that we have repaid it. Raimund Herincx opened the season with his wife, Astra Blair. I was at the piano. Raimund was a very busy singer at the time singing the main baritone operatic roles at Sadler's Wells (they had yet to rename themselves English National Opera). We enjoyed working together and toured around the country giving recitals. Looking back I am baffled how I did this. I was working in the City of London as an underwriter during the day, taking risks every minute—yet one of the most daring risks I was taking was the running of the RCS. I kept my touring schedule to the holidays, although I recall leaving my desk in the City one day at about four o'clock in the afternoon and catching a train down to South Wales, giving a recital, attending a post concert reception, catching a sleeper back to London, being awoken early, getting back to the City and starting work at about 8.30 in the morning.

Also at the community centre was the second concert of the 1966-67 season and this was a piano recital by Valerie Tryon. Valerie was making a great impression on the music scene. Not only was she a pianist with a superb technique but she had an innate musicianship which made her someone rather special. We found it difficult to agree on the programme she was to play but eventually settled for the Bach/Liszt transcription of the organ prelude and fugue in A minor, Beethoven's opus 109 piano sonata, and some Debussy and Liszt. I recall advising her on the colour of dress it would be desirable to wear—I suggested that white would be preferable so that it did not clash with the red curtains which covered up the tatty stage. Valerie played on ground level and she made an enormous impact on the audience. It was to be the first of many recitals this great pianist has given to the society.

That season we gave eight concerts and had 160 members. The subscription now stood at 25 shillings and for the first time we had a very small balance in hand. As chairman, I put forward my philosophy that we should attempt to build up reserves sufficient to pay all our debts should the society fail. Whilst we were not there yet, and it took some years to achieve this target, eventually we did it. This made financial sense to me although I found myself in conflict with fund-giving bodies who looked at reserves with distaste, but then they did not have to organise concerts and take the personal financial liability as well. It may not be appreciated that members of any committee may well be personally liable for their society's debts in the event of the society's collapse. This fact underlined my desire to build up the RCS's reserves to protect my colleagues.

There were a number of changes as we progressed to the 1967-68 season. The constitution of the executive committee was getting more stabilised and two newly appointed officers were going to make a major impact on the society in the next few years. Mary Cadman became the honorary secretary and Mark Moore the honorary treasurer. It was very useful to have Mary living a few streets away from me and for years we worked in close harmony. Mark Moore was the owner of the main record shop in Richmond. Richmond Records was indeed one of the most comprehensively stocked record shops in the west of London. Mark was a tireless worker for the RCS, although he was not the easiest person to work alongside. He could be prickly and dogmatic but a lot of the RCS's achievements over the next few years must be credited to Mark.

We changed the format of the brochure so that it could be opened out and used as a form of poster. The number of events increased from eight to ten and we increased the subscription to 30 shillings. Looking back on this season it represented good value for money, and the aims of the society were clearly stated as being:

1. To give public concerts of a high professional standard.
2. To give these concerts in the best possible setting.
3. To help create the right atmosphere for the enjoyment of music.

Although the wording has changed slightly over the years the sentiments of 1967 still stand to this day.

At long last I could do what I wanted to do as director of music. My desire was to explore the borough, gradually seeking out venues which were attractive and which had good acoustics. We didn't always get it right, and it became a case of trial and error, as acoustics are tricky to assess without an audience to absorb any over-resonance.

The new season started with a concert version of a Mozart opera *The Abduction from the Seraglio*—a wonderful score which was well sung by a cast that included Helen Lawrence in the difficult role of Constanza, Richard Gandy singing Belmonte, her lover, and Noel Noble as Osmin, who is always cast as a rather tubby Turk—so we needed some imagination as Noel was a lanky Australian! It deserved a far larger audience than it got. I felt at the time that it was a worthwhile experiment, and the passage of time has not changed this view.

Valerie Tryon returned, after her brilliant recital of the previous season. This time she gave the first performance in this country of Andrzej Panufnik's *Miniature Studies*. Andrzej had fairly recently moved into Twickenham at Riverside House, and I thought it would be a good idea to involve him in the life of a local, if struggling, concert society. He was invited to become a patron which he accepted. I provided Valerie with book one of the studies which

Valerie Tryon, a photograph taken by the author. Valerie has been a regular artist since the very early years of the society.

covered numbers one to six. I thought it was asking a lot to get her to prepare these technically very difficult and original works for piano. I also thought it would be sensible to ask her to come over to Twickenham and play through the first book to Andrzej. We went into Andrzej's studio, which had a large Steinway, and Valerie sat down and played the studies right through. Andrzej was staggered not only at her formidable technique but at her understanding of the music. When she finished number six she stopped and Andrzej asked her if, after a short break, she would like to play the other six which formed book two. She had to admit to him that I had not given her a copy, but she said she would have a look at them. Both Andrzej and myself were completely taken aback when she sight-read the book two studies without a fault. She went on to play both books when she gave the recital in the Waldegrave Ballroom in Horace Walpole's house in Strawberry Hill. She also gave a wonderful performance of Ravel's *Gaspard de la Nuit*, another work requiring great technique and musicianship. The critic R V Ward, writing in the Richmond and Twickenham Times, remarked that we as a society "could feel well satisfied with a concert, given under conditions that were first rate by any standards, by a young pianist who can be counted among the country's best". We were beginning to get it right.

We were still putting on a few events in private houses and it was necessary to keep these to members only. That season we had a master-class on lieder by Helga Mott at the then home of Mr and Mrs Dickson on Richmond Hill, and another event at the home of Edward Croft Murray on Richmond Green. Edward was a delightful man whom I got to know quite well as on occasions we travelled together up to London. It was on one such train journey that he asked me if I had always lived in the Richmond area. I replied that in fact I was born in Ludlow. He expressed surprise at that and told me that he, as he put it, had a pad near Ludlow himself and visited it when he was able. Many years later, after Edward's very sudden death, I went back to my roots and Monica and I decided to pay a visit to a National Trust property a few miles out of Ludlow. We discovered that Edward's pad was none other than Croft Castle.

Edward was the keeper of manuscripts at the British Museum and one of his eccentricities was to limit the music he enjoyed to a year or so of the Regency period in England. On the occasion that we visited number 4 Maids of Honour Row, Edward entertained members with his instrumental ensemble and talked about Richmond in music and pictures. So here we were in one of Richmond's historic houses which had been built in 1723. In 1744 it was acquired by "the ugliest man in London" whose portrait adorned a wall in the house. As this gentleman was acquainted with Handel it was not entirely beyond belief that the composer could have visited him. As the music was performed, drawings of old Richmond were projected on to a screen, and this added to the delight of those members fortunate enough to have got tickets.

To have the opportunity of visiting these marvellous houses was a bonus for members, but it caused a great deal of discord among those who could not get tickets. We now had so many members that we had to take the decision to reduce the number of members-only concerts, in order to counter the criticisms voiced by those members who failed to get tickets.

That season we included a string quartet concert by a well known quartet of the day—the Amici. It was also the first time we presented a concert at St Mary's church in Twickenham, which I have heard described by an eminent viola player as one of the best venues to play quartets in the country. They played Haydn, his opus 20 No 5, and the great G major quartet of Schubert, but the quartet that received the most emotionally involved performance was the seventh Shostakovich quartet.

Looking back, the 1967-68 season was a turning point for the society. I was able to get the committee's agreement to move concerts around the Richmond borough, and the criticism I had received previously that members would not go to concerts out of Richmond town was proved wrong. Members did come to hear some good music presented in more attractive surroundings, therefore as it turned out the risk was worth taking.

So as the swinging sixties started drawing to a close we presented our 1968-69 season of concerts, consisting of fourteen events, whilst still keeping the subscription at 30 shillings. We were on the move in more ways than one. We added new venues, such as the Cassels Hospital on Ham Common, and although the hospital represented exceptional value for money nevertheless we still wanted to cater for even bigger audiences than the hospital could accommodate. The committee was strengthened by Peggy Watson joining as refreshment secretary and by the addition of Gilbert Turner, the borough librarian, a lovely man who had been very supportive of the society although critical of the quality of our printing.

Mark Moore acquired for himself a Gestetner duplicating machine which he was quite prepared to put at the disposal of the society for the printing of programmes. So now I needed to type the programmes and the notes carefully onto a duplicating skin. For those who do not recall the joys of working with a duplicator I need only say that it was like typing on tissue paper and every mistake could only (in part) be corrected by using a pink solution. It was all very messy and the skin I presented to Mark was more pink than the original colour!

We opened the 1968-69 season with a violin and piano recital by Alfredo Campoli and Valerie Tryon, now a dear friend of the society. They had established themselves as a leading duo and the name of Campoli was indeed a draw. We presented this concert in the Lawrence Room of Cassels Hospital which could seat an audience of about two hundred. I would like to say that the concert went off without any hitch, but really I cannot. I had major problems with Campoli, mainly because he demanded that the piano be tuned to his pitch and the tuner told me that if this happened it could well cause a number of the strings to break. I had to make the decision to keep the tuning at the existing pitch. We had words backstage, not quite coming to blows but not far off. Dear Valerie acted as peacemaker and so, with a smile, I introduced this distinguished violinist to the audience who sat there in total ignorance of what had been happening backstage.

The recital was also an interesting one as we gave the first ever public performance of a work by Liszt. It was his violin sonata, in truth not a great piece but one worth the occasional performance. It was later recorded for Pye by Campoli and Valerie. At that time Liszt was still a neglected composer. Much work had been done to establish him as a figure to be reckoned with by such fine artists as Louis Kentner, but it was an uphill battle. I have always regarded him as a major figure of 19th century piano literature and without his influence much of the impact of Debussy, Ravel and Bartok would have been lessened. So I did what I could to bring his music to the RCS, not only in this concert but later in the season with an illustrated talk by another Liszt enthusiast, my friend Roger Wimbush, who wrote a monthly article for the Gramophone magazine. This talk was given at the home of Andrzej and Camilla Panufnik in Twickenham. We also presented two short operas—*The Music Master* by Pergolesi and Wolf-Ferrari's *Susanna's Secret*. This, I suppose, was the first anti-smoking opera as the secret Susanna had was her addiction to the tobacco plant.

Raimund Herincx and Astra Blair paid another visit in December of 1968 and the setting was the Waldegrave Ballroom. An Anthology of English Song was the title of the evening, and once again I was at the piano.

The critics gave the concert a good review—"notable song recital"—and we included some early English pieces by Thomas Campion and Rosseter and, to bring the recital up to date, a duet by Dennis Gray Stoll (youngest son of Sir Oswald Stoll) from his opera about ancient Egypt, *Songs and Dances of Karnak*. Dennis was a strange man. He was obsessed with ancient Egypt and the god Ra, and I recall when we were rehearsing the piece that Dennis seemed to go into a trance and swore that, for a moment, he became the god Ra himself. Later Raimund and I included some of Dennis' music when we gave a recital in the Queen Elizabeth Hall in London.

Looking back on 1969 I recall that one event created such a crush that we could not get everyone in. I accept that the room was not very large but I regard this particular event as almost the start of the public awareness of what we were trying to do. The irony was that it had very little to do with music. It was a rehearsed reading of *Under Milk Wood* by Dylan Thomas and we included the original musical settings of Daniel Jones; these were sung by the girls from Twickenham County Grammar School, under Doreen Hogarth who taught music at the school. How this came about was as follows. Some time before, Monica and I were asked to take part in a rehearsed reading of Dylan Thomas' masterpiece at the National Physical Laboratory, Monica's one time workplace. It was a great success and also a lot of fun to do. I thought, as we gave a number of these readings around the borough, that if we enlarged the scope of the evening by including the music, it would be worthy of presenting to the RCS. Alun Glyn Jones, then a curate at St Mary's church in Twickenham, took the pivotal role of First Voice. What happened was that the parents of the girls in the choir wanted to come and suddenly all the seats had been taken. People stood around the room and in the corridor outside, and it turned out to be a highly successful and most enjoyable evening.

We also had an orchestral concert which included Britten's *Les Illuminations* sung by Richard Gandy, and to end the season the chamber orchestra from the Royal College of Music came to St Mary's church and performed Britten's *Serenade for Tenor, Horn and Strings* with the young Martyn Hill as the soloist. The string orchestra was led by a young student, Levon Chilingirian, who went on to form one of the best known string quartets, who played for us in the late 1990s. I am still asking myself how we managed to arrange an orchestra in the small space between the choir stalls in this beautiful church! It was a good concert and the programme also included Elgar's *Serenade for Strings* and a short piece by Andrzej

A musical discussion in St Mary's church in Twickenham between our first president Andrzej Panufnik (on the right), Peter Lamb, another composer (centre), and the author.

Panufnik—his *Landscape*. The concert was conducted by Harvey Phillips who had some seasons before given a cello recital for the society.

So this almost saw out the 1960s. We had survived the personality problems of the early days and were now starting to have our own identity. The audiences were improving but the financial position was still tight. We had received that year £679.17s.8d and spent £693.19s.8d. Mr Micawber in *David Copperfield* would have said that this amounted to misery but we were far from that state of mind as we looked forward to the 1970s and to the dramas that lay ahead.

Chapter Three

HUNTING FOR NEW VENUES

During the 1960s—the period which saw the formative years of the Richmond Concert Society—the conditions in the country at large made life difficult and almost threatening. In 1962, when we started presenting concerts in Richmond, we were in the last two years of the Conservative government, a period when having turned our back on closer integration with Europe we saw ourselves almost left behind in the economic miracle which was taking place in Europe led by West Germany. In 1964 the Conservatives left office, and for a period of six years we had a Labour government led by Harold Wilson.

The problems which were gradually building up in the last years of the Conservatives erupted when Labour took office and we had the legacy of poor labour productivity, an unstable pound and, what became more and more a problem, trade union disquiet. In 1970 at the June 18th general election the Conservatives were returned to power under Edward Heath and their mandate was to take us into the EEC, to curb the growing power of the trade unions, and to do what they could to restore economic growth. This was a difficult period to live through. Edward Heath failed in his effort to curb the unions. He had to face up to a miners' strike, made much more effective by the oil embargo imposed by the Arab oil-producing countries. It was a period when not only factories but offices as well were reduced to working a three-day week, due to cuts in electricity supplies. All this had its impact on the Richmond Concert Society, not only in the problems of putting on concerts in these conditions, but in the demands that I had to face. My professional capacity was as an underwriter in credit protection, which required long hours at work (when one could work), with all power going down when electricity supplies were curtailed. Like others I had difficulties in travelling, and I needed to drive all over the country to advise major industrial companies on their credit exposures, and trying to save companies from going into liquidation—a process then in its infancy but which I was later to develop into what became known as "intensive care".

These conditions persisted more or less through the 1970s which saw Harold Wilson again failing to curb union power. Eventually he decided, very suddenly it seemed, to retire as prime minister and he was succeeded by James Callaghan, who also failed to control the ever growing power of the trade unions. It was a period of bitter disputes and by the end of the decade we had to suffer the winter of discontent which brought about the demise of the Callaghan Labour government and made way for Margaret Thatcher who became prime minister in May 1979. This decade was one which saw the RCS growing in size and quality, whilst the country diminished itself as it proceeded on what seemed to many of us a course of self destruction. This might seem strange, but it was possible that the Richmond public looked to the Richmond Concert Society as a place to hear music where they could, at least for two hours, put their concerns on one side.

We maintained the subscription at 30/- for the 1969-70 season and altogether put on sixteen events—a wide assortment of concerts, talks and opera films. It looked impressive on paper and generally it all worked out well. The opera scheme, which had been so well conducted by Patricia Hobbs, needed a new secretary as Patricia had decided to leave the area and move to Oxford. A fairly new member to the committee, a teacher, agreed to take over the administration of the scheme. At the start it worked reasonably well but later it created major problems for Mark Moore, in his capacity as treasurer, and myself as chairman—but more of that unhappy period later.

A valuable member of the committee at that time and for a number of years was Mary Kennedy. Mary had been with the RCS almost from the start and she took it upon herself to find new venues. It was Mary who discovered, a year or so later, St Margaret's Catholic church, which had been rebuilt after the war and proved highly satisfactory as a concert venue. I recall that on visiting the church for the first time I had my doubts about its acoustic worth. Really it should not work. The walls are made of concrete, the roof is at a low level where the audience sit rising to quite a substantial height above the podium where the fixed altar is situated. The amazing thing is that it does work and has served us well for many years.

Running a season of sixteen events needed a lot of commitment but the committee were fully up to the challenges presented. We opened in September 1969, with a membership of only 212 despite what we regarded as an attractive programme. By October this had increased to 267 but the number of members who had not renewed was high at 100. This compared with an opening membership the previous season of 136 which eventually grew to 253 by the end. A harp recital by the attractive Marisa Robles opened the season and her brilliant virtuosity was appreciated by the audience. Marisa was a strong personality and loved communicating with her audience despite the problems she was having with the English language.

The next month we had a members-only evening at Petersham House, which at that time had a reasonably large room at the back of the house and was ideal for small concerts. I remember, when trying to put together the new concert season, seeing in the Charing Cross library a brochure of the London Music Club announcing that Annetta Hoffnung was going to give a talk about her late husband, Gerard Hoffnung, who had died in 1959 at the age of thirty-four. In her biography of her husband, Annetta admitted that she "could remember very little about that talk, except my unbounded relief when it was all over". This was quite understandable as it was the first time she had ventured out as a speaker on this or any other subject. I decided to make contact with Annetta and she came and gave an illustrated talk, and recalls the event in her book. It was, as with the other talk she had given, quite a new experience for her and I believe that she gained a lot from her visit to the RCS. Afterwards we had quite a long discussion on how the talk could be improved, and a few further talks were set up at wives' groups, and as a result over the next few weeks and months she was able to polish her delivery. Soon Annetta felt confident enough for me to make contact with a concert agency, whom I knew well, and they secured a large number of bookings for her. Altogether she gave at least a hundred talks about Gerard all around the country, which certainly helped her financially.

There were so many interesting events that season that it would be impossible to mention them all, but in December we went to a new venue, St Anne's church on Kew Green. I remember only too well the meeting I had with Canon Clifford Pronger, who was the much loved vicar of St Anne's. He warned me that, for some unknown reason, various organisations had found it difficult to get an audience to come to St Anne's—he could not understand it. I told him not to worry too much as our members, I was convinced, would love to hear music in his church. He agreed to our using St

Anne's on the strict understanding that neither he nor the church were in any way responsible for any financial deficit arising from the concert. I assured him that in fact we would be making a donation to the church.

The first concert we put on in St Anne's was very much an occasion for two reasons. It consisted of a piano recital by a young British pianist, John Lill, who had recently won the Dinu Lipatti prize, and from the outset Clifford Pronger set out to make the whole evening an occasion. He had the church beadle welcoming the members as they entered St Anne's. There he stood at the entrance dressed in his fine costume, looking for all the world like Mr Bumble in *Oliver Twist*. This was, to the best of my knowledge, the last time the beadle, dressed in all his finery, appeared at St Anne's and I gather, when I enquired about the garment some years later, that it had disappeared, and nobody knew where it had gone. What a great pity, as it added so much colour to what turned out to be a memorable recital. John Lill played in his programme Beethoven's short F major sonata opus 54 as well as the great C minor sonata opus 111. He also played a Prokofiev sonata. The impact he made was considerable. I could sense from the audience that they felt that here was a pianist of stature. Only Valerie Tryon in her early recitals for the society made an impact as strong. I spoke to John at the end of the recital and asked him if he would be prepared to come again the next season for the same fee. He agreed but, by the time he performed again the following season, he had been to Moscow and won the Tchaikowsky prize, the most prestigious piano prize in the world. It was very much to his credit that he kept his word to us, despite the demands on his time which naturally followed his winning the Tchaikowsky. Whenever a pianist wins one of these famous competitions, such as the Moscow Tchaikowsky or the Leeds International, they are inundated with engagements for at least the next two or three seasons until the next prize-winner comes along. Personally, I look with some suspicion on these competitions and frequently find myself at odds with the distinguished panel.

In the Lawrence Room of Cassels Hospital we invited Eric Fenby, who acted as the amanuensis to the paralysed Frederick Delius in the last years of his life, to come and give an illustrated talk. Some time before, Ken Russell had produced his great television film about Delius. It was an outstanding piece of television. I recall asking Eric Fenby what he thought of the film. He felt that Max Adrian, who played the part of Delius gave so true and accurate a portrait that it completely bowled him over, and it was like reliving the nightmare months that he spent helping the paralysed composer. He was not so convinced about Christopher Gable who played Fenby himself, as he felt that he was too tall to impersonate him. Having Fenby in our midst, I felt, was living history.

We put on two films during the season—one, the Margot Fonteyn and Nureyev film of Prokofiev's ballet *Romeo and Juliet*, and later in the season a film of *La Traviata* with Anna Moffo. A dear friend of Monica and me, Michael Quinn, brought all his projection equipment to the Richmond community centre to show these films.

We have always tried to include within our programmes a lieder recital and this season Dick Gandy and Gordon Cumming gave a performance of Schubert's *Die Schöne Müllerin* at a new venue in the Maria Grey College (now Brunel University) in St Margaret's Road, Twickenham. At that time it was actually outside the Richmond boundary although a few years ago when boundaries were redrawn it just crept in. It was not totally satisfactory as a venue; however we did use it again that season when Bernard Roberts gave a piano recital which included some Beethoven, Mozart and the Aaron Copland piano sonata.

Dick Gandy, who not only gave many fine recitals for the society, but also became its chairman, a position he held for some years.

So the season drew to its close with the Arriaga String Quartet playing an all-Beethoven programme. After all these concerts we were pretty exhausted as the season drew to its end, but membership was creeping up bit by bit, and we were starting to make an impact on the Richmond borough's musical scene.

By the start of the 1970-71 season internal committee matters were settling down reasonably well, although there were clouds on the horizon with regard to the operating of the opera scheme. I had my reservations, mainly financial about the cash flow problems the scheme created. We had to pay out fairly substantial sums to the Royal Opera House to secure the discounted tickets in advance. We were finding that, despite the small subscription to become a member of the society and the good discounts we were able to negotiate with the Royal Opera House for the opera and ballet tickets, members were expecting the society to give them credit as well. Gilbert Turner, the borough librarian, a most useful and trustworthy member of the executive felt that we should take a tough line as we, frankly, did not have the money to lose should a cheque bounce. The opera secretary at the time felt that if we took a tough line it would make her job unpleasant and she would wish to resign. She felt slighted and after the meeting dear Mary Cadman, as secretary, received a registered letter from her to the effect that she felt that Mark, our treasurer, had implied that under her custodianship the whole opera scheme was in a mess. She wanted an apology, written or verbal, from Mark, which he refused, in my view quite correctly, to give. The result was that she resigned. It was a worrying time for all of us on the executive as the opera scheme accounts turned out to be as we feared. One evening, I remember it well, Mark turned up at my home with what account books he had managed to get from the opera secretary and for hours, well past midnight, we tried to put the books in some order and to ascertain just how much money was unaccounted for. At long last, and with great patience from Monica, we managed to get the books in a reasonable shape but there was quite a considerable amount still owed to the society. It took months and months to get the money from the opera secretary—a most miserable experience for all concerned. There was no question of dishonesty on the opera secretary's part, just a terrible muddle she had allowed to grow.

The 1970-71 season started out with a piano recital by Yonty Solomon. I am very fond of Yonty and he gave everyone a most enjoyable recital which included the second book of Chopin studies, as well as the same composer's B minor sonata. It attracted a large audience and I still do not know whether this was due to Chopin, Yonty or a mistaken belief that the great Solomon was going to perform.

I felt we touched history again when Imogen Holst, the daughter of Gustav Holst and also a great friend and assistant to Benjamin Britten, came and talked to the society in the Waldegrave Ballroom. She spoke with great love and admiration about her father, and traced his career from his early years in Cheltenham to the family living on the riverside at Barnes. In recent years Monica and I visited the graves of Benjamin Britten and Peter Pears lying side by side in the Aldeburgh cemetery and there, just behind their graves, is that of Imogen Holst. There was something pathetic about the position of Imogen's grave, that even in death she lay in the shadow of Britten and Pears.

Looking back over all the years, I must say that we have rarely needed to make new plans, but it did happen to us in October 1970. Some months before, I had negotiated with the distinguished violinist and teacher Frederick Grinke to come and give a recital with Joseph Weingarten, who had played with the Budapest Piano Trio in one of our early concerts. Alas it was not to be, as Frederick Grinke died after we had gone to press with the brochure. He was deeply mourned throughout the profession. Fortunately another good violinist, Maria Lidka, came to the rescue, in a duo recital with Peter Wallfisch, the father of the internationally known cellist Raphael. Perhaps, on reflection, Peter partnered Maria in the C minor violin sonata of Beethoven as if he was tackling the *Hammerklavier* sonata. Peter was a large toned pianist with a formidable technique whereas Maria's tone was small in comparison. I was grateful that it had been possible to find a substitute at such short notice, although musically the recital was less than satisfactory.

Again that season we listed sixteen events, of which most were live concerts although we had a film about the life of Mozart and another one with Beecham conducting Offenbach's *Tales of Hoffmann*. Once again our good and kind friend Michael Quinn operated the projector. Dick Gandy with Gordon Cumming gave a performance of Schubert's *Die Winterreise*, as always very musical and well worth hearing. So often in those early years we relied on the help and kindness of friends in the world of music. Such a one was Sidney Harrison, a lovely generous man, who as a student at the Guildhall School of Music and Drama won just about every prize worth winning in the 1920s. When years later Sidney died, his widow, also called Sydney but spelt with a y, gave me one of Sidney's prizes as a remembrance—this was his bound volume of Beethoven's thirty-two piano sonatas, a cherished possession.

Although I had the responsibility of being chairman and music director at this time, I was helped by a most supportive team. Mark Moore was full of new ideas, many of which we took on board, and some still remain in place today. Mary Cadman, as secretary, was a tower of strength during the opera scheme fiasco, as indeed was Gilbert Turner; I was going to need Gilbert's wise counsel at a later time.

As far as the creative side went we had to do as much as we could using talent from among the membership. Money was at the root of many of the decisions we had to take, and although we were making some impact on the musical scene, we were still running the society on very slender resources. In April 1971 I wrote a play based on the colourful life of Paganini, and assembled a cast made up of members from the Richmond Shakespeare Society and some other sources. The pivotal role was taken by my old friend Roger Wimbush, who was best known for a monthly retrospective article he wrote in The Gramophone. In the setting of the old town hall in Richmond the Paganini story was told with Mark Moore bringing in the music from his turntable just at the right moment. It was well received by the audience despite running for nearly two hours. Even though the critic said that it was "an absorbing evening", I have never written another play.

By the way, whilst recalling this Paganini evening I obtained from the Richmond library (no doubt with the help of the borough librarian, Gilbert Turner) a poster advertising a recital by Paganini at the old King's Theatre on Richmond Green in 1834, when he played some of his own compositions including one using just one string—a typical Paganini display of virtuosity. This certainly added some local colour. Incidentally, the same cast gave another performance of *Paganini: Man and Legend* in a concert hall attached to Raimund Herincx's home in Buckinghamshire some time later.

I have always tried to keep certain artists as, how can one put it, house artists. In the early days certain musicians made a deep impression on the society, and they came back several times over the years. The members felt that they got to know the artist, and it worked the other way around as well. Valerie Tryon came into this category as indeed did Bernard Roberts and Raimund Herincx. A month later, just after recovering from my Paganini, I was at the piano again in a recital with Raimund Herincx. This time we performed two substantial song cycles, both ideally suited to Raimund's dark-toned baritone voice. The first was the rarely heard *Songs and Dances of Death* by Mussorgsky, and the other was the deeply moving *Four Serious Songs* which Brahms had written towards the end of his life. To end the season John Lill fulfilled his promise made to me prior to winning the Tchaikowsky prize in Moscow, and gave a superb recital to a packed St Anne's church on Kew Green.

I think one could say, looking back, that this season established the society as a growing one in the Richmond borough, although certain storm clouds were starting to gather and they hung above us for some time before they broke.

The accounts of the 1970-71 season showed that we had increased our fees on artists from £416 to £540, and subscriptions had increased at an excellent rate—from £460 in the previous season to £713. So at the end of the season we were nearing our objective of creating sufficient reserves to see us through another season should a disaster befall. We very nearly had such a disaster with the opera scheme but, after much effort, received all the money back. So, at long last, we were no longer in deficit as we had an excess of income over expenditure of £222.

At the annual general meeting I had to report that the opera secretary had found it necessary "for personal reasons" to tender her resignation, which had been "regretfully accepted". What else could I say in the circumstances? Then from the floor of the meeting two ladies offered to assist in running the opera scheme. They were a Mrs James and a Miss Margaret Sims. Margaret, in particular, was to become a close and trusted friend and not only operated the scheme brilliantly, but during the next season met her future husband, Owen Smith, through the society. This was not the first time the Richmond Concert Society became a marriage bureau.

The original plan for the new season was to include Dame Eva Turner, the legendary Turandot at Covent Garden before the war. Eva came to one of our earlier concerts and she was always very helpful to me. Often I would phone her up and discuss certain musical problems I had encountered, and she would always be free with her down-to-earth northern common sense. I recall once going to the Coliseum to hear the English National Opera, and whilst waiting in the foyer I was embraced by this diminutive lady, which must have been quite an achievement for her. She never stopped working and even in her nineties she would commute by plane to the USA to give master-classes. It was a great pity that she could not come to the society due to her commitments on the other side of the Atlantic.

Just before the start of the new season The Richmond and Twickenham Times announced in a banner headline that "the Richmond Concert Society is very nearly fully subscribed" and, because we had to control the level of our membership to what the various venues could hold, it was a true statement. This problem has been one which has affected us throughout the past forty years. We opened the season with dear Sidney

Harrison talking about Chopin and playing many of this composer's compositions. He had a wonderful way of communicating with his audience and I am sure many members went away from that evening with a much greater understanding of why Chopin was so important in the history of music and in particular the piano.

Now almost a resident pianist, the ever popular Valerie Tryon played again for the society in October 1971. Valerie was then, and continues to be, one of the most outstanding interpreters of the music of Liszt. She has the formidable technique to cope with every technical problem Liszt could write—but she has the innate musicianship to make sense of any music she plays. Later the Hungarians were to honour her with the Liszt medal, an honour bestowed on only a very few distinguished musicians, such as the conductor Georg Solti. Well, on this occasion two things stand out in my memory. One was that she included Liszt's great B minor sonata and according to the critic she gave "a towering performance and how right she was to go so deeply into its structure and emotive motivation." It really was a great performance but strangely Valerie dislikes playing the sonata and, if she can help it, never includes it in her concert programmes. This is, as I have tried to explain to her time and time again, a mistake but I must accept that if she dislikes the piece then don't perform it. The other thing I cannot forget was the fallout after she read another critic writing about the same recital. He wrote: "One might describe Miss Tryon as a petite figure, if comparing her to many other women pianists. Nonetheless, her force and resilience, her power of attack, and her ability to maintain it in full flow, are prodigious and astonishing. If one closed one's eyes, one might have presumed it was Mr Tryon who was on the platform. Altogether a performance to warm the blood and long to remember." One might think this was a good review of a memorable recital but Valerie, always a feminist, disliked the comment about "Mr Tryon". I calmed her down—eventually— but I needed all the tact in the world to achieve it.

As I have said earlier there have been very few concerts which have gone wrong in that the artist, for good reason, could not perform on the agreed date. This is understandable and normally you have some time to find a replacement, but on one occasion I booked a young Australian pianist to give a recital in the Waldegrave Ballroom in Strawberry Hill. I tried to make contact with him some weeks before, in order to get the programme finalised, but no response, and it was with only about a week to go that I discovered, quite by accident, that he had decided without telling anyone to return to

Australia. With very short notice a good friend from my Guildhall days, Benjamin Kaplan, stepped in and gave a delightful recital. Ben, whilst a finalist in the Liszt competition, never really had a career as a concert pianist but he became one of the great piano teachers with an international reputation, and achieved a lot over the years to raise the standard, in particular, of young Japanese pianists. We still phone each other up when the Leeds piano competition comes on television and compare views on the various contestants, and whilst we agree basically with each other's views, we find ourselves in disagreement with the so-called expert panel of judges on the first three or four places.

That season we also had to do another quick fix as John Culshaw, who produced that superb Solti recording of Wagner's *Ring* for Decca could not, at the last moment, come and talk. On this occasion Peter Gellhorn came on to the platform, and talked and played, mainly from memory, great chunks of Wagner's *Ring*, trying to explain what this monumental work is all about. It was a remarkable tour de force.

Marisa Robles performed again—there had been little improvement in her English since she had last performed for us, but it was as always a fine performance from this generous spirited harpist.

At that time, and for some years afterwards, there had been on television a programme called Face the Music where the quiz master was Joseph Cooper. It was at the time a hit programme and Joseph became a household name. His speciality was his "hidden melodies", where he took a well known song and disguised it in the style of one of the great composers. It was an amazing feat. I thought it would be a good idea to invite him to the RCS, as I was sure he would be a success, and another inducement was that he lived locally on Barnes Common with Jean his wife and his beloved cats. This love of cats brought us very much together.

I fixed this up with one of the major agents of the day, Ibbs and Tillett, and the person who looked after his engagements was a young girl called Carol Borg. Carol was a delight and we always got on very well. We fixed up that Joe Cooper would do his evening on Schumann and agreed the date as the 23rd May 1972 in Ham Hall. It attracted a good audience and Joe sat at the concert grand we had imported and began to tell the touching story of Robert and Clara Schumann—a story which I have over the years related in countless programme notes.

Then a magical thing happened. Joe was talking about the piano concerto Schumann had written and started playing the opening theme, which is for solo piano, and then, as if from nowhere, an orchestra started accompanying him as he proceeded to play the rest of the rather long first movement. What had happened was that off stage his wife Jean operated a special tape of the concerto, minus the piano part, and as soon as Joe had finished the few bars of the opening theme she did her part and brought the orchestra in, rather in the same way as a conductor, except her instrument was a reel-to-reel tape recorder.

Joe Cooper became a good friend to Monica and myself and although he came again to the RCS some years later, in the intervening period Joe had to face up to a personal tragedy.

By the close of the season our membership had increased to the very healthy level of 325. We needed now to give more attention to the presentation of the society in two major ways, one the design of the brochure for the new season, and the other to get someone to design a cover for the programme and the notes, which I had continued to write on stencils for Mark to duplicate on his machine. The design that we adopted for the programme cover incorporated a picture of a harpsichord with the words Richmond Concert Society wrapped around the instrument. It was printed on hard card and in three basic colours. The brochure design proved excellent and we kept with it for a number of seasons. It consisted of music stands in outline with the name of the society in white against a coloured background.

The 1972-73 season started with a recital by Moura Lympany and she gave a brilliant performance of the second Rachmaninov sonata as the highlight of her recital. We were, as usual, looking for new venues and Mary Kennedy had an uncanny gift for finding possible places we could use. We wanted space and we decided to put the Lympany recital on in St Mary's College chapel in Strawberry Hill. We received, as always, a great deal of co-operation from the college authorities but really the chapel, whilst perfectly acceptable for choral concerts, proved to be far too resonant for a nine-foot concert grand piano.

For the next concert we decided to use St Margaret's Catholic church, which was, as mentioned previously, a venue which had been discovered by Mary Kennedy, and to put on there a concert comprising a guitar, oboe and piano. This concert came about in the following way. Once a year an organisation known as the Greater London Arts Association auditioned a number of up-and-coming musicians, and after some sifting had been carried out they invited representatives of various organisations to go to the Purcell Room on the South Bank and hear these young musicians. A number of young hopefuls were listened to, including a young soprano who showed considerable talent—her name was Felicity Lott and mentally I put her name down on my list. On this occasion I was impressed by a guitarist known as Anthea Gifford and a young oboist, by name Malcolm Messiter. They were both engaged by us and over the years they achieved considerable success in their careers. There was also a young pianist who impressed me. I decided that he was well worth an engagement and he shared the programme with Gifford and Messiter. His name was Howard Shelley, and his deeply committed performances over the years on the international scene fully justified the faith I had in him at that very early stage in his career.

I was looking for a singer to give a recital in St Anne's church on Kew Green. It so happened that Monica heard a broadcast and fell, in a big way, for the voice of Benjamin Luxon. I made contact with his agent, but, to be honest, he showed very little interest in coming to the society. I persisted, or rather Monica bullied me into persisting, and eventually Ben Luxon came and gave an excellent recital with David Willison. He admitted to me that he really enjoyed singing for us and found the audience so attentive.

In those days informal talks formed a small part of each season and we invited the percussionist James Blades to talk to us about his varied life. Jimmy was a born entertainer and held the audience in the palm of his hand all the evening. He called his talk Recipes from an Orchestral Kitchen. Jimmy Blades was an extraordinary man—very approachable and a delight to be with. He came with his wife Joan, and I recall she had cut sandwiches for the occasion which he could have with his tea brought in a vacuum flask, all very homely. They were a delightful couple. It was Jimmy Blades who was the musician who tapped out the Beethoven "Fate" theme, which was broadcast by the BBC to occupied Europe during the war. He provided the sound of a gong which was heard at the start of hundreds of J Arthur Rank films, although he was careful to point out that the very muscular man shown hitting the gong was not himself but Bombardier Wells. He was also closely involved with Benjamin Britten. Jimmy was always very inventive especially when Britten wanted a particular sound and an example comes to mind. When Britten was composing his church parable A Burning Fiery Furnace, he required the sound of an anvil to sound like a bell in an Anglican church. He put his problem to Jimmy, who thought about it and came up with the idea of using a spring from an old Rolls Royce, which produced exactly the sound Britten had in his mind. Well, on this occasion he had the audience enthralled with his stories, and I remember very well one member leaving in the interval so that she could get her husband, who was at home, back for the second half.

Of the fourteen concerts that season all were live apart from Jimmy Blades' evening and an evening which was devoted to recordings by our new president, Andrzej Panufnik. Unfortunately both Andrzej and Camilla were ill in bed with flu, and therefore missed the evening but the sound of the new recordings, which had come out on the Unicorn label, was most impressive in the acoustic of St Mary's church in Twickenham.

We invited Antony Hopkins, who was such an outstanding communicator on music, to come to the Cassels Hospital to "Talk about Music". I tried and tried to get him to commit himself to a particular theme or topic but to no avail. He wanted freedom to talk on his theme, whatever that might be on the night. The result was that I did have a problem with the evening, as I discovered chatting to him before the concert started. He had decided, without telling anyone, that he would play a sonata by Schubert which had just been discovered. This would have been fine, but as it happened we had just had a performance of the same sonata at our previous concert, when Peter Wallfisch had made a return visit. Antony Hopkins was completely thrown and went out on to the platform and said something about talking to an A-level audience, or something like that, which a lot of members took exception to, with justification. It was not a happy evening although I remember that Antony sat down at the piano after everyone had gone home (except the committee) and sitting with his back to the keyboard played a few bars of the A major sonata of Mozart—it was his party trick. Clearly he felt rather guilty about his conduct as he went out of his way to offer to come back again that season, at no fee. This time it was given in the drawing room of Toby Jessel's home near to Hampton Court.

The season came to an end with a piano recital by Anthony Goldstone, a highly gifted but strangely neglected pianist.

At the annual general meeting that year Mark Moore as treasurer was able to announce that although our subscription income had declined by £20 we still had an excess, although small, of income over expenditure.

In the April 1973 budget the chancellor, Anthony Barber, introduced a new type of tax—the value added tax, which although a new concept of tax collecting effectively replaced the old purchase tax. It had a direct bearing on our overall finances, which had not been touched to any great extent by purchase tax. The new tax made a significant impact on artists' fees, piano hire and printing costs. We thought hard and long at the time whether we should register and thereby claim back the tax we paid, but the administration required to do this was not one any voluntary treasurer was prepared to take on.

The new season, which started on the 2nd October 1973 began with very much a celebrity piano recital by the great Shura Cherkassky. Shura was an extraordinary man, somewhat eccentric but lovable too. He insisted on a special diet of fruit before playing and was very fussy on how he was dressed. He also wanted us to hire a second piano so that he could practise right up to the moment that he went out to give his recital. This needed some tact, as we could not afford an additional piano. Hiring one piano was expensive enough. A member of the committee, Phyllis Huggett, offered her piano to Cherkassky as she lived very close to the church. This extracted us from what could have been a tricky position. I was intrigued by his hands as they resembled those of a furry animal, so covered were they by a thick coat of hair. A Cherkassky recital was always something of an experience—you never quite knew what he was going to do. It was what one

Shura Cherkassky, one of the great pianists of the "old school". One never knew what Shura was going to do next, but his recitals were always memorable.

might describe as inspired piano playing. The story was often told that when he was rehearsing a concerto, and the conductor had eventually got used to his waywardness on tempo and in the process had got to the point of despair, Shura would get up from the keyboard after the rehearsal had finished and tell the conductor, to his horror, "Don't worry, I will play it quite differently tonight!"

He was one of the most exciting pianists I have heard, very much one of the old school of piano playing—he had an amazing technique, but this was secondary to his ability to communicate with his music. On this occasion he performed one of his favourites, the *Wine, Women and Song* waltz by Johann Strauss II in that incredible transcription by Leopold Godowsky, and the *Pictures from an Exhibition* by Mussorgsky. The audience which packed St Anne's church in Kew loved every moment. It was a concert to remember, and only recently a member who was at that concert came up to me and said what an experience going to that Cherkassky recital had been.

Later in the season we had one of those rare hitches when the string quartet booked to appear—the Fitzwilliam—for some reason decided that they could not do the concert. I had to find another quartet as quickly as possible. At that time, having a close connection with the Greater London Arts Association (who went into liquidation a few years later), I sought their help and they strongly recommended the Medici Quartet, who were still studying at the Royal Academy of Music. They came and were quite outstanding. As a quartet they went from strength to strength appearing all over the world, a success well deserved. I like to think that we gave them one of their first engagements, and for many years they were one of the most exciting young quartets on the circuit.

Some months earlier Monica and I had dinner in Twickenham with Raimund Herincx and his wife, Astra, together with Joseph Cooper and his wife, Jean. So successful was their appearance the previous season that they were booked to do a programme about another composer, this time Tchaikowsky. The formula was to be much the same with Joe playing the piano and doing the talking, and Jean coping with the recording equipment by the side of the stage. The dinner was a happy affair as we all got on so well but Jean took Monica aside and said that she had a problem, which she had kept from Joe, because they had been asked to perform at Windsor Castle in front of the Queen. She was aware of a lump. As it turned out she had cancer and died a short time before the April 1974 concert for us. Joe was distraught and I recall speaking to him for a very long time on the phone and he was shattered by Jean's death. There was no way he could undertake the Tchaikowsky evening without Jean being there to provide the necessary background, and anyway he was emotionally drained. I had to look around for a replacement. This was not easy because, of course, Joe Cooper was at that time a household name and any substitute needed to be in the same category.

With the help of Carol Borg at Ibbs and Tillett I was able to get Cyril Smith and Phyllis Sellick to give a recital. Some years before, on a visit to Russia, Cyril had suffered a stroke which rendered one arm useless. With great courage Phyllis and Cyril managed to get many of their two-piano compositions rearranged, without losing any notes, for three hands. This clearly put a great technical strain on Phyllis, but being such a fine pianist, she coped. It was another memorable concert and I was indebted to them both for cutting short their holiday in Cornwall to rescue the evening for me. As it happened, a short time afterwards Cyril had another stroke, this time a fatal one. The concert for the RCS was therefore one of the last concerts ever given by this brilliant and regretfully underrated English pianist. Cyril, before his first stroke, had a fine technique and his recording of the third concerto by Rachmaninov on 78s was quite outstanding and remains clearly in my memory.

That season we put on thirteen events and most of them attracted good audiences. By this time the subscription had risen to £2.50, which still represented good value for money considering the quality of artists such as Cherkassky and Craig Sheppard, the second prize-winner of the 1972 Leeds competition, who also performed for us.

At the January 1974 meeting of the executive committee it was my pleasure to welcome on to the team Owen Smith who a few weeks earlier had married our opera secretary, Margaret Sims. They had met in the RCS and I was delighted for them both. Owen was going to be a great asset to the society in the seasons to come, and when he died in his nineties he left a small legacy to the society. In his last few years he was looked after with great care at the Royal Star and Garter at the top of Richmond Hill.

It was about this time that I happened to meet, in Richmond, Isador Caplan, whose wife, Joan, had been on the committee for a number of seasons, and was indeed one of the founders. Isador and Joan had allowed their house at the top of Richmond Hill to be used for member evenings in the past, and were always very supportive of the society. Isador told me about the Richmond Parish Lands Charity, of which he had been made the chairman, and suggested that we made application to them for a grant. We applied and received what was at the time a substantial sum of £275, which in today's values would be nearer £1,600. Our debt to this wonderful charity knows no bounds. They have helped us, and many other organisations, and it would be true to say that without the financial assistance we have received from them our growth would at best have been stunted.

It was around the early 1970s that the RCS was involved in cross fire between two stubborn individuals, both of whom happened to be friends of mine, which made life, to say the least, difficult. I can touch very briefly on what occurred and the impact it had on the society. Mark Moore, as mentioned earlier, had an excellent record shop in Paradise Road, Richmond. It was first class in almost every way, good stock, a central position in the town, etc. But it did have a problem because Mark was not particularly customer friendly. He would look at you over his beard and his half glasses and put the fear of god into you. It was really an intimidating business to buy a record from him. On one occasion a man, who happened to be a patron of the RCS, went into the shop and asked for a record, which Mark did not have in stock. He asked if he could order it and Mark said that he could but he wanted full payment for the record there and then. The man took objection, turned around and walked out of the shop. I am sure such slight differences of opinion happen frequently in day-to-day transactions in shops, although I would like to think that we are more customer orientated these days.

It was a pity that a few days later a letter appeared in a local paper complaining about the treatment that the writer had received in Richmond Records. Mark in turn felt aggrieved about the letter, asked for an apology and none was forthcoming. Solicitors were consulted, and as Mark seemed to love nothing better than being involved with the law, the whole matter, so it seemed to me, went into a steep decline. I tried my best to get the two parties together so that the matter could be discussed and hopefully solved in a civilised manner but to no avail. I was informed that effectively, if I got rid of Mark from the committee of the RCS then concerts would continue to be reviewed in the local paper, but if he was allowed to remain then no publicity or review of any concert would appear. I confided in my old friend, Gilbert Turner, and we both felt that the society was being held to ransom on a matter that did not concern us in the least. The decision that I took, rightly or wrongly, was to back Mark.

As the dispute got past the solicitors stage, it eventually started heading for the law-courts! How it was resolved I never discovered for certain but I believe it was eventually settled out of court. The only winners, as is frequently the case in these stupid disputes, were the legal practitioners.

What I do know for certain was that the amount of publicity or reviews that we felt the society relied upon, whilst still appearing, were at a lower key than hitherto—yet the society grew at a more rapid pace than before all this unfortunate business happened! If I heeded anything from this stupid episode it was that press coverage does not really count for much if one has a good product to market. We felt that we had precisely that. The fact that we were providing what the musical public wanted was having an effect not only on our membership but in the level of audiences generally.

The 1974-75 season again had a number of jewels including a fine Chopin recital by Tamás Vásáry and an organ recital by that doyen of church organists, George Thalben-Ball, in the Richmond parish church. I had a problem on how best to project an organ recital. Once the organist was on his seat, away from sight, a recital could well become an uninteresting depersonalised affair. I think it was solved with George Thalben-Ball coming out in front of the audience and having a chat with me about the pieces that he had decided to play. This audience contact did the trick and the recital seemed to work.

A most unusual concert was held at St Margaret's Catholic church in November 1974. I had the idea of inviting the flamenco player, Paco Pena, and frankly did not know what hit me. By and large the traditional membership stayed away, but I had not reckoned on Paco's following and the church was packed to overflowing. At the end of the concert there were shouts from around the church of "Olé!" and I don't think we have ever sold so many non-member tickets, before or since, than we did on that evening.

This was also the season when we encountered funding problems with the National Federation of Music Societies. We had been members since we started and had received small grants from them. They now started laying down the law as to the level of subscription that we had to levy on members. We opposed such interference and eventually Mark and I went up to the London offices of the Arts Council of Great Britain, no less, and met representatives from the National Federation and the Arts Council, and, to put it mildly, we had a stand-up row. Even after all these years I can still recall the scene with the Arts Council and National Federation on one side of the desk and Mark and myself on the other. Neither side was prepared to give an inch. We valued our independence and our right to apply the level of subscription we required to run concerts, and as a result received no grant that year or any other year since. I have often asked myself the question "Were we right to take the stand that we did to make the RCS concerts available to all?" I am convinced that the stand we took was the correct one and I believe, had we buckled under to bureaucratic pressure and increased the subscription, that the RCS would not be alive today.

Felicity Lott came and sang at the Waldegrave Ballroom, and John Ogdon gave a recital which included a Tippett sonata and the Liszt B minor sonata. We encountered problems at a late stage with this concert as John's agents, Ibbs and Tillett, had double booked him and when he was supposed to play for us he was still in America, so we had to have the concert a day later. After the concert at a small reception at the home of one of our patrons, Vaughan Hoad, I was aware, although I did not realise it at the time, of John's mental illness. He sat in the background on a couch glowering, speaking to nobody—so unlike this large, kindly man. The sadness of John's illness and the effect it had on his career has been well documented, so I won't dwell on it here.

At the end of the season, really at the insistence of the Richmond Parish Lands, we invited a well known group of the day, the Philip Jones Brass Ensemble, to perform in the terrace gardens on Richmond Hill. To present any concert in the open air can be a delight, if everything goes right, but being England it can incur weather hazards so we presented it on a June evening. The evening was fine and the concert possessed its own charm. I wanted the concert to have an impressive background with lights colouring the trees. It looked magical. The five brass players set up their stands some distance away from the trees at the bottom of the terrace gardens and played. A breeze gently blew and it was sufficient to blow the music off the stands. Everything was taken in the best of spirits and the audience sitting on the grass on such an evening basked in the sound of Gabrieli and other masters of brass music. Often when I met up with Philip over the years we would have a good laugh about this concert. Philip, the gentlest of gentlemen, died in the early part of 2000. He had a habit of wearing the most colourful ties that he could lay his hands on, and when at his memorial service the brass ensemble performed they all wore brightly coloured ties. Precisely what Philip stipulated in his will.

For the 1975-76 season the subscription was retained at £3, possibly as an act of defiance against the Arts Council of Great Britain. I do not regret for one moment the stand we took against this august body, who almost set themselves up as god where the arts are concerned. Later I heard of other societies, similar to the Richmond Concert Society, who behaved themselves and increased their subscriptions in line with the arts council's directive only to find a dramatic drop in membership. Regretfully many societies ceased operating as a result.

The new season had a number of highlights. Rafael Orozco, who had won the Leeds International Piano Competition in 1966, gave a recital which displayed plenty of piano pyrotechnics but, to my taste, left one wanting more from an interpretative point of view. Valerie Tryon returned after an absence to give a wholly satisfying recital, strong in technique as well as musical intelligence.

In March 1976 Gervase de Peyer came with Gwenneth Pryor, a most underrated pianist from Australia. It was to be the first of a number of concerts given by this impressive duo. On this occasion Susan Daniel, a young soprano who had fairly recently married Gervase, sang among other items that wonderful aria from Mozart's *La Clemenza da Tito* which requires a clarinet. Susan, who had sung a convincing Carmen at Richmond Theatre for Gemini Opera, had been relentlessly pursued by Gervase. The problem that evening was trying to keep the peace between Gervase and his young wife, who seemed to be having differences of opinion. They separated some months later.

April marked the first appearance of the internationally acclaimed Music Group of London. The violinist was Hugh Bean, the cellist was Eileen Croxford, who later became a close friend of Monica and myself, and the pianist was Eileen's husband, David Parkhouse. They performed the Beethoven *Archduke* trio, a work they became very associated with and which they recorded around about that time.

David was one of the finest chamber music pianists I think I have ever heard. He, like so many English pianists, was much underrated during his short lifetime. The other outstanding concert of that season was the last one, a piano recital by Vlado Perlemuter. When Vlado was on form he was a most sensitive interpreter of Chopin, Fauré and Ravel. He was the only living pianist who had studied the entire piano music of Ravel with the composer, so when he came to St Margaret's Catholic church in June 1976 one felt very close to musical history, and we were very privileged to be present. Vlado's major problem was memory lapse. This was possibly due to his experiences during the Second World War when he suffered badly under the Germans. I was with him just before his recital at St Margaret's church. He was terrified of going up the twenty or so stairs to reach the platform. His manager, Basil Douglas, and I virtually had to take one of Vlado's arms each and carry him up the stairs.

The membership of the society had slipped a bit from the previous season and now stood at 380, but the society was financially on a much sounder basis than in the critical early years.

Mark Moore was involved with the twinning of Richmond with Fontainebleau in France and Richmond in Virginia, and as a French week had been organised for late September 1976, it was felt appropriate to have a French pianist to open the new season. Mark had heard a young pianist called Didier Picard and he was invited to start the season off. This concert was an exception to my own golden rule—that I must hear for myself any artist we decide to engage. On this occasion I followed Mark's recommendation, but as it turned out the recital was not a success. Picard proved to be a rather dull pianist who needed a great deal of attention. Our dear friend at St Margaret's Catholic church, Father Desmond Swan, had to provide a bath in his house which was by the side of the church and generally fuss around him. He seemed a rather unbalanced young man, so I was not really surprised when I heard some years later that Didier had committed suicide.

Peter Katin came on his first visit to the RCS in November and gave a memorable Chopin recital. The following month, in the parish church in Richmond, we heard the second performance of the new string quartet by Andrzej Panufnik played by one of the leading quartets of the day, the Aeolian. Over the years we programmed all the fine string quartets that Andrzej composed.

I remember vividly Felicity Lott's second recital for the Richmond Concert Society, as it was on the 7th December. Once again that fine accompanist Graham Johnson was at the piano and the concert was in Kew church. Benjamin Britten had died two days before and I thought it would be appropriate to pay tribute to him by including one of his songs in the recital. I spoke to Felicity on the phone and she agreed with me that it would be fitting to include a short tribute to this great English composer. At the end of the recital she sang the folk song setting which Britten had made of *O Waly Waly* and everyone in the audience was deeply moved. Over the past forty years there have been many wonderful moments that come to mind, but of them all

Felicity Lott's singing of this simple folk song must stand at the top of the list.

Moura Lympany came again in May 1977. She had been made a patron of the society after her earlier recital, and it was always a pleasure to hear this great artist perform.

Right at the end of the season we welcomed back Joseph Cooper. In 1973 Jean, his wife, died and you will recall how distraught he was. In 1975 Joe secretly married Carol Borg, who had been his agent at Ibbs and Tillett. It was then with considerable pleasure that we were able to welcome him back on the 7th June 1977 to give a concert which had an air of celebration about it as it marked the 25th anniversary of the Queen's accession to the throne. Joe described the event in his autobiography which he called, very appropriately Facing the Music:

"On the 7th June practically everybody in the country must have had their eyes glued to their television set, because it was the day of the Queen's silver jubilee. On that day I was doing my musical stint for a local organisation, the Richmond Concert Society, run by the enterprising Howard Greenwood, who has built up Richmond Concert Society into one of the leading music clubs in the country.

"Carol and I thought this might be a good chance to try out the idea of the play and talk programme she had suggested. I started with serious talk and classical pieces and progressively made the programme lighter. I finished by playing hidden melodies—the melodies were often tunes from musicals or the 1920s and 1930s which the audience sung lustily. I asked Howard Greenwood what he felt about the mixture; he said the audience had thoroughly enjoyed themselves and loved the opportunity of being able to give tongue. I might add we had started the whole proceedings by singing *God Save the Queen* and that evening it seemed to have a special meaning.

"Emboldened by Howard's encouragement I played a similar programme to a packed Queen Elizabeth Hall, London, on Bank Holiday Monday, 16th April 1979."

It had been a most rewarding season and to end on this note of festivity seemed appropriate.

Mark Moore had some months earlier indicated that he wished to relinquish the role of treasurer and retire not only from the RCS but also from Richmond. It had always been his intention to retire to the place where he was born, Malmesbury in Wiltshire. So we had plenty of warning in order to find another treasurer. I knew that Mark, for all his odd ways, was going to be difficult to replace. Not only did he look after the financial side but he did much else as well. He did all the printing of programmes from the stencils I had produced. From the start I had always written programme notes to assist, as far as I was able, the enjoyment of music heard. As season followed season soon the programme notes started to be more expansive. The end product, with the programme content encased in an attractive cover, looked good, but one could never really produce a quality programme using such an old-fashioned method of reproduction. To be honest the actual programme looked amateurish, but we could not afford anything else at this stage.

Peter Katin opened the 1977-78 season playing with his usual elegance the Beethoven *Pathétique* sonata, and the great B minor sonata of Chopin. As always Peter drew a large audience. The other pianist that season was the veteran Louis Kentner, at the end of his very distinguished career. No pianist did more than Kentner to bring to the musical public's attention the lesser known works of Liszt. Gone to a large extent was the brilliant glitter of his earlier career, but it was wonderful just to have Louis with us and the audience responded to this great musician.

The singer that season was the young Yvonne Kenny who sang in the rather resonant acoustic of the Richmond parish church. She was then at an early stage of a brilliant career which took her to Glyndebourne and the major opera houses of the world. I recall some problem getting Yvonne to send me a programme. She was singing at the Edinburgh Festival and there was no way that I could make contact with her. I knew that she had worked with John Amis recently, so I phoned John to see if he knew where I could make contact. He wrote back, with his usual wit: "Sorry, can't help. Can you ask someone at her flat to go through her drawers?!"

Celebrity concerts came one after another. Evelyn Barbirolli came with Iris Loveridge; Gervase de Peyer made a return visit with Gwenneth Pryor; the Coull String Quartet played; and to end the season we had, for the first time, a harpsichord recital by the great George Malcolm. George was the complete musician. Not only was he a brilliant harpsichordist, but an organist, as well as one of the foremost choir trainers of his day at Westminster Cathedral. Benjamin Britten had written his *Missa Brevis* for him, and he had conducted the London Symphony Orchestra in the recording of Britten's *Cantata Academica*. His recital was a memorable experience but I do recall one slightly amusing incident. The concert was held in St

Margaret's Catholic church and as George completed the first half of his programme, instead of returning down the stairs to the room set aside for him, he got completely disorientated and approached the exit door leading to the garden and tried desperately to open it. As he struggled, I gently pointed him in the right direction.

The 1977-78 season had the new treasurer replacing Mark Moore. Harry Curwen was a great character. Larger than life, he looked very military with his impressive moustache, and a winning, wicked glint in his eye. What a find! Harry had had a distinguished career in the tobacco industry and had received the MBE. He certainly added presence to the society and I was grateful for him and his solid good sense.

I look back on the 1978-79 season with some satisfaction as I was able to bring to the society two outstanding pianists—Jorge Bolet and, on a return visit, Shura Cherkassky. These pianists were among the few remaining pianists from the golden age of piano playing, and it was a wonderful opportunity to hear them both within a few weeks. Jorge had a great reputation as a Liszt player. His recordings on the Decca label of Liszt received rave notices, and became classic recordings still in the record catalogue today. I had admired him since my youth. He had produced the piano music for a film about Liszt which starred Dirk Bogarde and then had virtually disappeared. When I heard that he was going to visit this country again, I made every effort to track him down to engage him for the society. We became good friends and I spent a whole day with him when he recorded for the BBC the complete *Transcendental Studies* of Liszt. At the concert there was some misunderstanding which only became apparent as we climbed the stairs at St Margaret's Catholic church for Jorge to make his entrance. I mentioned that I was looking forward to hearing him play the Franck *Prelude, Chorale and Fugue*. For a second he paused and said that he was unaware that he was starting his programme with this piece, as he expected to start with a Mendelssohn prelude and fugue. "Not to worry, Howard," he said. "Although I have not played the Franck for about two years, I will start with it if the programme says so." And he did and gave a superb reading of this work. He also played the twenty-four preludes of Chopin.

The next concert was also something unusual and is still remembered by many members. It was called "Dancing through the Ages" and consisted of music dating back to the days of the troubadours up to the 17th century. Ancient instruments were used and the performers wore the costumes of ancient times and danced literally all around the Richmond parish church.

Then the next month we had a return visit from Shura Cherkassky. This time it was in the main hall of York House (Clarendon Hall), and Shura was in his usual great form. Seeing him before the recital he was in a highly worried state—very concerned with a pin-sized dot on his white shirt. "What will the audience feel," he said to me, "when they see the black dot?" "Don't worry, Shura. I can barely see it myself so it is hardly likely anyone in the audience will see it." This seemed to pacify him. I felt that he needed to hype himself up just before going on to the platform.

In January 1979 the Music Group of London came, this time without Hugh Bean, the violinist, but with the oboist Keith Puddy, and they played the Brahms and Beethoven clarinet trios. Howard Shelley, who you will recall impressed me at a Greater London Arts Association concert some years before, now had a recital to himself and played an all-Chopin programme. I would put Howard as one of the most brilliant of English pianists. Some years later he had a terrible accident and put his hand through a sheet of glass and had to have all the nerves and tendons operated upon. He still conducts and plays concertos wonderfully, but it is sad that he no longer gives piano recitals.

It was a season of twelve contrasting concerts and those which I have not specifically mentioned were all, in their own way, quite outstanding.

The last few concerts of the 1970s brought the decade to a close in an impressive manner. The Chinese pianist Fou Ts'ong opened the 1979-80 season. I recall that he was unhappy with the Steinway and could hear a buzz on one of the strings. I must admit that I could not hear it myself but it was necessary for the Steinway tuner to take the piano to bits to try and cure whatever it was that upset Fou Ts'ong. I forget now what it was, except that it was difficult to cure, because the tuner really did not know what he was looking for, as he also failed to hear the buzz.

A month later the St Margaret's Catholic church was packed for the master-class which was given by Jacqueline du Pré. This was arranged in conjunction with the Richmond upon Thames Arts Council but it was very much a Richmond Concert Society event. I arranged for three young cellists to subject themselves to Jackie's views on interpretation. The whole concert was given in aid of the Jacqueline du Pré Multiple Sclerosis Research Fund. We were never certain whether the event would take place or not—it all depended on Jackie's health at the time and whether or not she was going to be in remission. As it happened she was able to carry out the engagement and I wheeled her in and out of the church. It was a deeply moving occasion as poor dear Jackie talked and talked, being quite unable even to touch her beloved cello.

The other concert at the end of 1979 was given by the young violinist Nigel Kennedy. He came with Yitkin Seow and it was wonderful to hear and see two young and highly talented musicians loving not only working together as a duo, but enjoying each other's work. This was the only concert that I can recall where the performer, in this case Nigel Kennedy, asked if it would be possible to sit in the audience, to hear Yitkin play the Chopin preludes.

The 1978-79 season was Mary Cadman's last season as honorary secretary of the society. Mary was a tireless worker for the society and was totally committed to seeing that we survived. I could always rely on her when one crisis was followed by another. She gave stability to the executive committee and I knew that I was going to miss her support, although she always said that she would continue to come to the concerts. She was made a patron and a life-long member, and if anyone earned these accolades Mary did.

And so the decade of music-making had come to an end. We had established ourselves, and the problems of the early part of the 70s had gone. The year 1979 had been quite eventful for the country at large and we had not only established ourselves within the Richmond borough but had also become in Joe Cooper's words "one of the largest music clubs in the country".

Chapter Four

SPONSORSHIP TO THE RESCUE

The last chapter saw the society establish itself, not only within the Richmond upon Thames borough but within the musical profession, as one of the country's leading concert societies. The problem that faced us in the 1980s was—could we maintain the impetus?

In running a society such as the RCS one cannot ignore the world outside. Unfortunately it was not a happy place at all. As we moved into 1980 the country had to brace itself to face a major steel strike. There was a 3,000-strong army of flying pickets, based in the Yorkshire area, set to strike at the private steel sector, and as this produced some 20% of the country's steel this was clearly a worrying development. As an underwriter in credit, with a major responsibility for the steel and engineering industries, I was at this time under a great deal of stress. I commuted on a regular basis to the Midlands and the North, the centres of these industries. The level of industrial strikes was appalling with some 29 million working days lost, three times that of the previous year. Not since the general strike of 1926 had the country been so paralysed.

The chancellor in 1980 was Sir Geoffrey Howe who produced an austerity budget of sorts which tried to combat the other major problem facing the United Kingdom, that of inflation. By April that year inflation had burst through the 20% barrier and there was no sign that it was going to fall—rather the reverse. With costs rising at this rate the financial pressure on the RCS was the same as for everyone else—extremely worrying.

So it was a period of great instability and unrest which affected all of us in our respective workplaces. As the chairman of the TUC warned, "The net result of the government's period of office is already clear—hyper-inflation, industrial degeneration and social conflict" and that just about summed up the situation, although many of the problems really emanated from the over-powerful trade unions throughout the country.

Somehow, in all this industrial chaos, the RCS not only kept going, but saw a record growth in subscriptions as membership soared to 530, which was really too high for the capacity of the halls and churches we used for our concerts. Whilst it does give some force to the argument that during periods of strife the public turns to the arts for some degree of sanity and comfort, this membership growth nevertheless needs some explanation. The fact was that many had subscribed to the society just to have the opportunity of hearing the legendary Jacqueline du Pré, whose master-class had taken place earlier in the season.

For my own part I had difficulty in keeping myself going, let alone the society, as travelling to all parts of the country trying to save companies from going bust was starting to take its toll on my health. As a result I really had no option but to give up the position of chairman. The problem was to find someone to take it on. I had served thirteen years in the dual roles of chairman and music director and every member on the executive committee, including myself, wanted someone at the helm for the next period of activity. I asked my old friend Dick Gandy if he would become chairman, and to be quite honest he was most reluctant to take it on. However, Dick thought about it and after some months eventually agreed, on the understanding that I remained as the director in charge of the concerts, which I agreed to do. He took on this role, so he said to Monica and me, purely out of loyalty to the society. I was deeply grateful to him and for the next few years we worked alongside each other in reasonable harmony.

The rest of the 1979-80 season also had a number of concerts of interest. In January we had an enjoyable visit from a male vocal group called the Scholars, and they are still around in 2002 but mainly as a recording group. It was a period when vocal groups seemed to flourish with the King's Singers leading the field.

In February we invited Music Deco, which consisted of a singer, the mezzo-soprano Meriel Dickinson, a saxophonist, Christopher Gradwell, and a pianist, Christine Croshaw. In March the Myrha Saxophone Quartet, led by the great saxophonist John Harle, came to St Margaret's Catholic church. I look back on these two concerts as the RCS's "saxophone period". The Meriel Dickinson concert included a performance of *The Song of Surabaya Johnny* by Kurt Weill which has remained vividly in my memory. I have never heard anyone else interpret that moving song as well as Meriel did that evening. It was sheer magic. Some years later, at the English National Opera, Meriel gave a memorable performance as Mrs Jones, that monster of a gossip-monger, in Kurt Weill's *Street Scene*.

Towards the end of that season Ian Partridge and his sister Jennifer performed Schubert's song cycle *Die Schöne Müllerin* at St Anne's church on Kew Green to great acclaim. Rightly Ian and Jennifer's interpretation of this wonderful cycle has for years been praised, and their recording still stands as one of the most satisfactory I have heard of this great work.

And so the season drew to a close with a recital by Peter Frankl. Looking back I feel that my enthusiasm for the piano music of Schumann and my desire to share it with members of the society went somewhat out of control! I asked Peter to perform all the piano sonatas of Schumann in one recital—there are three altogether. Now, certainly two of the sonatas are fine pieces, the sonatas in F sharp and G minor, but to have all three sonatas in one programme was, in retrospect, gilding the lily. Not inspired programme building on my part!

Another outstanding British pianist opened the 1980-81 season in September and that was Imogen Cooper. She played the Beethoven *Pathétique* sonata and also a Schubert sonata. Imogen tends to concentrate on a particular project and around the early 1980s she played a lot of Schubert, and made memorable recordings of a number of the sonatas. The impact she made on the audience was such that I made a mental note that she would have to return another season.

Some years previously we had mounted a concert performance of Mozart's *Seraglio* and it was during this season that we put on in the Richmond parish church a costumed performance of *Cosi Fan Tutti*. I would count this a reasonable success but nothing more—some of the singing was frankly not up to the standard that we have always tried to achieve, but certainly it was attractive to watch.

I was excited that I had been able to persuade Jorge Bolet to return and play again for us, and in December he came and played two major works. All the first half was taken up with a performance of the four scherzi of Chopin. These work as a group, despite the fact that they are not in any way linked musically. Jorge, as ever, gave wonderfully compelling interpretations of these Chopin pieces, and in the second half played the Liszt B minor sonata. This unfortunately was to be the last time Jorge played for us. His career was a strange one, as it took him a long time to achieve the recognition he so rightly deserved. He was for many years what one could call a pianists' pianist, as exponents of the keyboard the world over have testified. It took him a long time to get known in this country, possibly because of poor management representation. Once his Liszt recordings on the Decca label were released they helped his career a great deal, and years later they are still in the record catalogue as classic performances. During his autumnal years, he was at last recognised in this country for the great artist that he was, and was able to attract capacity audiences to the Queen Elizabeth Hall and Royal Festival Hall whenever he played. I was saddened to hear, a few years later, that he had died from an AIDS-related illness. He looked very stern when he mounted the platform and I always thought that he looked more like a doorman at the Royal Opera House than a leading concert pianist, but he was such a delightful man to know—very friendly and with a warm personality.

We invited an excellent cellist, Alexander Baillee, to give a recital in March 1981 and he played a Beethoven sonata, the exciting Shostakovich cello sonata and the Debussy sonata. It was Sandy Baillee, as he was known, who had agreed with Susan Dorey, to be pupils at the du Pré master-class held the previous season.

Dick Gandy and myself, in an effort to conserve funds, gave a lieder recital at St Margaret's in April. I recall this recital well as we started with the *Erl King* of Schubert. Why Dick wanted to start a recital with the *Erl King* continues to baffle me. It might make an effective start to a recital, but it is tough on the singer and, as generally accepted, near suicide for the pianist. There you are, coming on to the platform with the customary nerves, sitting down at the keyboard and starting to play the rapid triplet octaves of this great song. Now to keep this tempo up page after page is an exhausting business, as the physical pain starts in the forearm at about the end of page two. You know that you have a number of pages ahead of you, with the agony rapidly getting worse before Schubert introduces an arpeggio figuration in the right hand, which at least gives you some muscular respite—but it is only temporary, as back you go to the triplet octaves again. At the end of the song when the erl-king has caused the death of the child I think he can add the pianist to his list of conquests. There are ways to cheat by playing broken octaves in the right hand but being a devil for punishment I decided to play it as written. We also included in this recital Fauré's cycle *La Bonne Chanson*, a beautiful work not performed as often as it should be. Some English songs by Roger Quilter, which Dick loved to sing, completed the programme. The recital went well and the press said some kind things about Dick and me—and they are always pleasant to read! "The great success of the Richmond Concert Society cannot, of course, be directly attributed to having fine musicians as chairman and music director, but it helps. On Tuesday at St Margaret's, East Twickenham, Richard Gandy, tenor, and Howard Greenwood, piano, had as much to offer in their recital as many of the highly paid artists the society usually invites." Home-grown produce was being appreciated at long last! Dick Gandy was really a most musical singer, and we worked well together. We all have our own peculiarities and Dick was no exception. After every rehearsal I would receive a long letter from him tabulating every point of interpretation we had discussed at the rehearsal. This was fine as far as it went, but Dick's writing was very small and almost impossible to decipher. We both held strong views as to the interpretation of German, French and English songs but, strange to relate, rarely came to blows.

We welcomed back in May that year Vlado Perlemuter and again he played well—unpredictably but well. As always with a Perlemuter recital, I was sitting on the edge of my seat anticipating some memory lapse but, thank goodness, it did not happen. I remember collecting Vlado from St Margaret's Catholic church and bringing him home so that he could rest before the concert. He had very little English but was a delightful companion, and Monica and I tried to communicate with him in our halting French. I drove this old artist back into London after the recital and I seem to recall that despite his age he did a fair bit of flirting on the back seat with his lady companion.

Then to bring the whole season to a close we had an exciting young string quartet, the Endellion, and with Andrew Watkinson as leader it was a concert which kept up the standards that we always tried to reach. The Endellion played for us several times in seasons to come and they became, with every justification, one of the most outstanding of the younger generation of English string quartets.

That season we had made another move to improve our brochure presentation by using an attractive painting by Philip Mercier of Kew Palace with King George II's children playing musical instruments on the lawn in front of the palace. The painting is known as *The Music Party,* and we cut it down to show just three and not four of the king's children. We also used the same painting as our programme cover and this continued, using various colours, for some seasons to come. I think it remains my favourite of the

The illustration that we used on our programme cover for many seasons. It is from a painting by Philip Mercier (1707-1757). It shows the Prince of Wales and two sisters in front of Kew Palace. A third sister on the right in the painting was omitted.

various paintings we have used over the years in our efforts to make the brochure more attractive and the programme presentation more professional. We were still reliant on the stencil method of reproduction, which was the cheapest system we could use. To photocopy the programmes at that stage would have been prohibitive.

The 1981-82 season also saw the introduction of sponsorship. The first two sponsors that appeared in the brochure were the company I worked for, Trade Indemnity plc, and a brokering company known in those days as Sedgwick Forbes. With the continual round of one company taking over another, names change but these two sponsors, now known as Euler Trade Indemnity plc and Marsh Ltd, continue to support concerts to this day.

How did the question of sponsorship first arise? In the previous chapter you will have read of the problems we had with the National Federation of Music Societies and, in the background, the Arts Council of Great Britain. As a result of what they did we were effectively starved of funds. I think it is a generally acknowledged fact that the arts have always needed money to survive. The Arts Council of Great Britain try to be an independent body but are effectively government controlled. The solution, according to the National Federation who are funded by the Arts Council, was always the same—make a substantial increase in the subscription and then they would look more kindly on providing some money. We even had a visit from the secretary of the National Federation at one of our Kew church concerts, and his only contribution was to comment that many in the audience could well afford a very substantial increase in the subscription. This might have been true in certain cases but there were many who were not so well off and regarded their evening at the RCS as one of the month's highlights. Whilst we have always tried to be realistic on the level of subscription, it was felt by the executive committee at the time that to increase it ten times (which was really what the National Federation wanted) would effectively destroy the society and all the hard work and commitment so many had contributed over the years. We were hopeful that the local authority, through their voluntary grants sub-committee, would support us, as the Conservative council had done for the first years of our existence—but it was not to be. Application forms were completed, which took hours, only to have our request turned down year after year, on what seemed a whim and without any appreciation of what this truly voluntary society was doing in the borough. I had supposed, in my innocence, that the voluntary grants committee was there to help voluntary organisations such as the Richmond Concert Society—but I was in for a shock.

It seemed that the Richmond Lib-Dem council were not geared to supporting the arts in the borough despite all the rhetoric the politicians voiced. As matters turned out the only arts activity the local politicians seemed to understand, or indeed appreciate, was the theatre. They had no sympathy for serious music in the borough although the audiences that we were gathering in, at least on a nightly basis, were larger than the audiences going to the theatres. It was very frustrating, as we failed to get the voluntary grants sub-committee to understand that the Richmond Concert Society was in fact an artistic flagship for the Richmond upon Thames borough. On one occasion, I sat at the back of the salon in York House whilst the sub-committee pontificated on the grants they were prepared to give this organisation or that, and heard that we were to receive not a penny. To make matters worse, I heard one councillor, looking very anxious at the end of the meeting, making some enquiries as to why a particular jazz group had not put in an application—the inference being that if they were to apply they would get funds. We were starved of funds yet that particular jazz group, I gathered later, had ceased operating. It was all a bit of a farce.

To return to our original sponsor, Sedgwick's credit side was run at that time by a delightful man called Graham Heard. We had many battles over credit matters, and I always loved negotiations in which he was involved. He had a good legal mind, being a barrister, and for years we were good friends, which is a somewhat rare thing in the City of London. At long last I was able to persuade him that Sedgwick's could well benefit from supporting an up-and-coming concert organisation such as the Richmond Concert Society. Gradually I started to get my point across and Graham agreed to support us. In truth, over the years that he was involved as a sponsor he never missed a Sedgwick sponsored concert and loved each one. We frequently spent the two hours after a concert at Bellini's in Richmond for a relaxing post-concert dinner.

The 1981-82 season was the first one when the new secretary Denise Latimer-Sayer was in control, and a very fine secretary she was—a most efficient and delightful person all rolled into one. It was sad for me to say farewell to Mary Cadman, who as secretary for so many years had done a wonderful job. Denise had worked alongside Mary for the previous season so the hand-over of responsibilities was accomplished very smoothly.

It was a strong executive committee with Dick Gandy at the helm as chairman, Denise as secretary and Harry Curwen as treasurer. Owen Smith, who had married Margaret Sims, the highly efficient opera secretary, was a useful member of the committee and made himself responsible for getting the brochures around the borough libraries. Celia Curwen, Harry's wife, also contributed a lot with her knowledge of music. Muriel Dawson, who had first come on to the committee in 1971, was another valuable member of the team.

We were aware in 1981 that Margaret Smith was ill with cancer, and after a few months she died. It was a great loss to all of us. She had had a few years of blissful marriage to Owen, and we gave what support we could to him at this time of loss. The opera scheme, which had given so many of the members an opportunity of hearing opera at the Coliseum and Covent Garden at affordable prices, was to remain active for the remainder of the 1980s under various opera secretaries such as Miranda Burgess and Eileen Beer, but there could never be a replacement for Margaret Smith.

Valerie Tryon, always a favourite pianist with members, gave a recital of Scarlatti, Mozart, Beethoven, Brahms and Liszt which opened the 1981-82 season. It matters not what composer she plays as she has an instinctive grasp of each composer's style. She has a particular love for Scarlatti and listening to her playing some of the one-movement sonatas is a particular pleasure.

The well known and loved mezzo-soprano Sarah Walker came and gave a recital with Roger Vignoles in October. This was the first concert sponsored by Trade Indemnity, and I have always been grateful to the chief executive of the company at that time, John Phillips, for agreeing to sponsor. Despite the company being taken over years later by the French, they have continued this sponsorship support to this day.

Only very rarely have we had a concert by a choir but in November 1981 we had one given by the New London Singers. I mention this really for one reason because, in order to make the concert more acceptable, I introduced a young and unknown pianist, Barry Douglas, whom I had heard perform and who struck me as a performer with a large talent. He played two short groups of solos, including a Scriabin sonata and Chopin's *Polonaise Fantaisie*. Barry, a delightful Ulsterman, was some years later in 1986 to stun the musical establishment, including the Russians, when he took part in the eighth International Tchaikowsky Piano Competition and carried away the first prize. This was the second time we had spotted an outstanding talent at an early stage, the other one being John Lill.

During this period we were very piano orientated. Bernard Roberts, another of our regulars, came and played the last three Beethoven sonatas—a very demanding evening on performer and audience but well worth it. As Robert Harris, who reviewed the concert, said in the Richmond and Twickenham Times: "This was an event in which the normal criteria of criticism have to be discarded; best described, perhaps, in monumental understatements like that of Mr Roberts, who remarked to me after the performance 'They listened, didn't they?'" This remark of Bernard's has been repeated time and time again over the years as artists have expressed to me how attentive they have found the audience at Richmond Concert Society events, and I have always responded that the Richmond Concert audience was among the best in the country.

We invited the Bedfordshire Youth Chamber Orchestra to the society in April 1982. I had been very impressed with the standard of these school-children when I had heard them in the Royal Albert Hall. Like all orchestral concerts it needed a lot of organising but it worked. For a young orchestra to play Andrzej Panufnik's concertino for timpani, percussion and strings was no mean feat, but they performed it with credit and to Andrzej's satisfaction. The soloist in a Prokofiev violin concerto was Andrew Watkinson, who was leader of the Endellion String Quartet. They had played for us earlier in that season in most impressive performances of quartets by Haydn and Mozart and of Schubert's string quintet, which was the first occasion we had programmed this great chamber work.

Looking back on that season there was no doubt that we had some wonderful music-making but also a couple of concerts I would prefer to forget!

The 21st anniversary season opened on the 29th September 1982, with a violin and piano recital by a distinguished violinist of the day, Manoug Parikian, who came with Bernard Roberts. The theme of this season was the many sides of Beethoven. Altogether there were nine concerts and the emphasis was on quality of concert presentation. The Beethoven theme was taken up in the first recital when Manoug Parikian performed the *Kreutzer* sonata—a concert which was described by the Richmond and Twickenham Times as "a night to remember" and indeed it was. Manoug was a player of great refinement and all the sonatas in the programme were performed with consummate artistry. I recall the wonderful performance of the violin sonata by Elgar, a late and deeply felt composition dating from the end of the First World War. I made a mental note, listening to this performance, that this was a work I would like to programme again at a later date, and this I was able to do in the 1990s.

Peter Katin made a return visit in October. This was his second visit to the society and it attracted a large audience who gathered in St Margaret's Catholic church to hear Peter play a programme dedicated to the music of Chopin. We tried out an interesting experiment that season by running two string quartet concerts over two consecutive months. The idea was to present two of the late Beethoven quartets, and the ones we decided to programme were the F minor opus 95 and the C sharp minor opus 131. They were played by what had become almost a resident quartet, the Endellion, and as usual their playing was immaculate. Robert Harris, the critic, commented at the time that he recalled "casting a rueful eye a few years ago at the small audience attracted to a local concert by a celebrated string quartet", and wondered where was the audience? He gave the RCS the credit for the change and concluded that it was the way we actually marketed the concerts by having a unifying theme. I don't know whether this was true or not; I am more inclined to think that musical tastes had started to change and if we had any skill at all it was an awareness that this was happening. So it could be said that the two Endellion Quartet concerts of December 1982 and January 1983 were landmark events, as audiences crowded into St Margaret's Catholic church and St Mary's on the riverside in Twickenham to hear string quartets. I could not help recalling the early stages of the society when my idea of putting on even one string quartet evening was viewed with some scepticism.

To close the season we had a piano recital by Martino Tirimo, and it was to be the first of many recitals by this very fine artist. Martino is a man of immense charm and has become over the years a close friend of Monica and myself. Looking back it is odd how we first came together! As one could well imagine, any music director of a society such as the Richmond Concert is inundated with brochures from this pianist and that, from singers ranging from sopranos to basses, from violinists—the list goes on and on. It is always sad for me to read and cast away so many of these expensive brochures when I realise how much money has been spent on producing them. But this casting away regretfully is a fact of life. The responsibility of any music director is to ensure, as far as budgets allow, a programme of excellence, so

Martino Tirimo, a wonderful pianist and friend whose recitals showed great sensitivity combined with a brilliant technique.

that any member of the public deciding to subscribe to the society can feel that they are getting value for money. Well, in the case of Martino I received a letter from his manager, who happened to be his wife, and I was intrigued by the address, which was a number of houses below where Monica had lived in Southfields before we married. Who was this pianist Martino Tirimo? I gathered from what was sent to me that he was the winner of two major piano competitions in Munich and Geneva some ten or so years previously, and I was also sent long-playing records of him playing the two substantial piano concertos by Brahms. I was really impressed with what I heard. Here was a pianist with a great sense of the architecture of these two major concertos, and I was quite intrigued that the tempo he chose for the first of the concertos was more measured than normally heard. As the movement developed the logic of this tempo became clearer to my mind. Wanting to hear him live, I decided to attend his next Queen Elizabeth Hall recital. The result was the May 1983 engagement when he performed the *Eroica Variations* of Beethoven and gave certainly one of the most poetic performances I have ever heard of the *Études Symphoniques* of Schumann.

By this time the subscription was £8 a season which, making some allowance for inflation, would equate to approximately double this amount in 2002. It was a season which I think one could look back on and say that it set the standard for what was to come.

Encouraged by the success of the double string quartet concert concept which we tried out in the previous season, we decided to repeat the experiment, only this time with a new and brilliant young quartet—the Coull. The theme behind these two concerts was the clarinet quintet. Now there are two outstanding classical clarinet quintets, the one by Mozart which we invited the veteran clarinettist Jack Brymer to play, and the one by Brahms which we gave to the very young player, Michael Collins, who went on to scale the heights of his profession. Michael had won the BBC Young Musician of the Year competition on television with a performance of the Finzi clarinet concerto, and indeed had put this attractive piece on the musical map. Both the Mozart and Brahms clarinet quintets received exquisite performances. Jack Brymer was a delightful personality and great fun to work with, and had the gift of being able to identify himself with the audience.

The 1983-84 season had opened with what had become almost a tradition—a piano recital—and on this occasion we invited the Australian pianist Leslie Howard to perform. Leslie is a very fine player who has made a speciality of the music of Liszt. By the year 2000 he had completed a massive project for Hyperion Records by recording everything, and I mean everything, Liszt had composed for the piano. It has taken him years to complete and numerous compact discs. I had heard Leslie give a recital at the Wigmore Hall of the waltzes which Liszt had composed. I thought it would be a good idea to have this unusual item in an RCS programme. Leslie has amazing energy and would play all night, if allowed to. The first part of the programme consisted of some Mozart variations and Beethoven's *Les Adieux* sonata and then in the second half the Liszt waltzes, which seemed to go on and on. The problem with so much undiluted Liszt is that you soon get indigestion in a big way. Again unusual, but I must admit not very brilliant programme building on my part!

However, another concert that worked very well was one dedicated to Edward Elgar. I have always been a lover of Elgar's music but the amount of chamber music he wrote is really rather limited. He turned to chamber music at the close of World War I when he had taken a lease on a small cottage in Sussex called Brinkwells. The idea was to include all the three chamber works belonging to the Brinkwells period in one concert. I had a word with a close business friend, Andrew Neill, who was at that time the chairman of the Elgar Society, and he generously supported the concert financially.

We held the concert at the German School in Petersham. The previous season we had tried out this venue and found it most satisfactory. For the Elgar concert, I seem to recall something went wrong and we were unable to use the platform for some reason, and so had to give the concert with the artists performing on ground level. The best laid plans sometimes go astray and although we had performances of the string quartet and the piano quintet, we had to substitute some short violin and piano pieces for the violin sonata, which was a pity. The Medici String Quartet played for us that evening and the excellent pianist was John Bingham. They were fully inside this idiomatic music as they had recently recorded the quartet and quintet.

The last concert of the season was a return visit from Martino Tirimo. This time he played the Beethoven *Waldstein* Sonata and the Schumann *Humoresque*. Again his playing of the Schumann convinced me that he was an outstanding interpreter of this composer. Martino has always played a lot of Beethoven including all the five concertos in the Queen Elizabeth Hall, which he directed as well as played, and in 2000 he performed the major task of playing all the thirty-two sonatas in a number of recitals at St John's Smith Square.

By the time we had reached our 23rd season in 1984, the subscription had increased to £10 and the number of concerts had stabilised at nine, and it seemed that we had a strong season to offer to members. By this time we had been successful in attracting sponsors for five of the nine concerts so things were looking up. Apart from the original sponsoring companies—Trade

Sharing a joke during the interval of a concert. John Ould is on the left, with Colin Squire, one of our sponsors, on the right. The hysterical one is the author.

Indemnity and the Sedgwick Group—we were able to attract the interest of Credit Insurance Association, Michael Cox Electronics Ltd and Squire's Garden Centre in Twickenham. Colin Squire has ever since been a great supporter of the society. He is always so enthusiastic and appreciative at every concert his company sponsors, especially if it involves the piano which he loves.

As mentioned earlier, in designing any new season we tend to introduce new performers as well as welcoming back certain artists who have established a close relationship with the society. Peter Katin opened the season with performances of a Haydn sonata and the *Appassionata* sonata of Beethoven where Peter's assured technique served him well, but it was perhaps in his performance of Debussy's *Estampes* that he reached the heights of pianism.

A new group played in the Richmond parish church in November and once again we questioned the suitability of this venue. It has certain advantages in that it is in central Richmond, with a commercial car park close by, but the disadvantages, in my view, outweigh what few advantages it possesses as the acoustic tends to be over-resonant with a loss of musical clarity. The Villiers Piano Quartet was a marvellous ensemble. With players such as Ian Brown, Maureen Smith, Susie Meszaros and Alexander Baillie it could hardly fail. They performed three great piano quartets by Mozart, Schumann and Brahms. Ian has been for many years the pianist of the Nash Ensemble and has played a number of times for the society. We did something during this season which we had not tried before, and that was to invite two of the players of the Villiers Piano Quartet to come back later in the season to give a violin and piano recital. This close association with particular artists and the members of the society has worked well over the years and clearly they loved hearing again Maureen Smith, an excellent violinist, and Ian Brown, possibly one of the best chamber music pianists, in a programme which included sonatas by Mozart, Prokofiev and Brahms.

The 1984-85 season was really quite a star-studded one with concerts by Michael Collins, the clarinettist who had been the BBC Television Young Performer of the Year, appearing with his regular partner at the time, the excellent Kathryn Stott; the Medici Quartet playing Haydn, Shostakovich and the second *Rasumovsky* quartet of Beethoven; John Amis, who gave an illustrated talk on his life in music remembering Sir Thomas Beecham, Percy Grainger, Gerard Hoffnung and many others; and Meriel Dickinson, who came with her brother, the composer Peter Dickinson, and as always it was a delight to have them with us again. To end the season, we welcomed another old friend, Bernard Roberts, playing two Beethoven sonatas and that exquisite last sonata by Schubert. In all it was a worthwhile season, giving a great deal of pleasure to the large audiences who were coming to the concerts.

In November we had an excellent piano recital by Howard Shelley and in January a visit from what was then a young forward-thinking wind ensemble, the Mladi, formed and led by Michael Collins. All the members of this wind ensemble were excellent players and the programme, if you happen to enjoy wind music, was delightful. The problem with having a whole evening of wind music is the lack of suitable repertoire. On this occasion we heard the very fine wind quintet by Nielsen as well as one by Françaix but on the whole the music, however brilliantly performed as it was on this occasion, lacked any real interest.

What I have learnt over the years is never relax over any season of concerts—you might regret it—and we had to be on our toes for two of the events scheduled in the 1985-86 brochure. Two concerts had to be rethought and for quite different reasons. We had advertised a talk by Sidney Harrison on "My Life in Music" for the February slot. It would have been a memorable evening as Sidney's career in music was fascinating both as teacher, performer and in later years as a television personality. I know Sidney was looking forward very much to coming back to the RCS but it was not to be, as he died a few weeks previously. We decided to turn the February date into a memorial concert for Sidney, who was a patron of the society, and asked Angela Hewitt to give a piano recital. This would have pleased Sidney who was a great admirer of Angela's playing. I had known Angela for some time past as each year, just after Christmas, Sidney and Sydney Harrison had a

Sidney Harrison, a brilliant pianist, teacher and author whose illustrated talks to the society drew large and appreciative audiences.

small party in their flat just off the Chiswick High Road, and Angela was often one of the guests. I asked her if she would give a memorial recital and she agreed without hesitation. Angela played Bach's fifth French suite and she has a way of playing this composer which is quite outstanding. It was little wonder that in the years which followed, Angela's reputation as one of the foremost interpreters of Bach was consolidated. She made a marked impression on the audience and I decided that at a suitable time she must return.

The other concert which went wrong, and I don't know why to this day, was one to be given by John Shirley Quirk, his wife Sara Watkins and the harpist Osian Ellis. I had been approached by Sara Watkins, who was quite a forceful personality, to see if a concert could be arranged. John and Sara lived in Strawberry Hill and they wanted to perform locally. It was all agreed but I admit that I found it difficult, if not impossible, to get any programme details from them, and then without any warning they decided that they did not want to give the concert at all. I was less than pleased but there was little that I could do at that late stage. Fortunately, that fine mezzo-soprano Sarah Walker stepped into the breach and gave a delightful recital with the up-and-coming Malcolm Martineau. Sarah has a great presence and a large personality, and singing Schumann's *Liederkreis* she was able to convey the many moods of this song cycle. I have always been insistent that whenever we put on a song recital, we provide the audience with translations of the poems. On this occasion, so great were Sarah's interpretative powers that really translations were superfluous.

We were asked if we could put on a concert for the Richmond Festival and we obliged by putting on a string quartet concert a month after the annual general meeting had been held. At that time Richmond had a reasonable festival but it seems to have disappeared for one reason or another, possibly because those who started it all decided to retire.

So the 24th season closed with the Endellion String Quartet playing in St Mary's church in Twickenham a programme which included a Haydn quartet, the Smetana first quartet and the G major Mozart quartet. We had kept the concerts to nine and the subscription had remained at £10.

At the annual general meeting the treasurer, Harry Curwen, who had taken over from Mark Moore, retired. He had been a fine treasurer and was a delightful man with his military bearing and very keen sense of humour. Now, we have always tried to operate a system whereby when one of the officers decides to retire his or her successor would effectively shadow the position for a season. Gradually the retiring officer would hand over the reins to the successor, and this has worked very effectively over the years. This happened with Harry the previous season, and for this season Paul Bowen, a man of wide musical experience as a conductor and critic, took over from Harry. Not only did Paul assume the role of treasurer, but using his skills on the computer we were able to start improving the ways we presented the programmes.

It has always been our custom to try and keep the level of subscription unchanged for a number of years, and then increase it by a reasonable amount rather than increase it each season by a much smaller amount. Nevertheless the fees for artists increase each season as do the costs of piano hire and hall hire. However, as we are very much a voluntary organisation, we do not get involved in high administration costs. So when we started the 1986-87 series of concerts we were able to keep the subscription at the level it had been for the last few seasons—£10.

As matters turned out it was a highly eventful season, and I would like to mention just a few of the excitements that arose during the course of the nine concerts that made up the season. We started with a harp recital by Marisa Robles. She is always a very warm personality on and off the platform but despite the years she had been in this country, her English, just as on her last visit to the society, still left much to be desired. I think she decided to practise her English on us rather than demonstrate her considerable ability as a harpist, as she did a lot of talking, mainly about her health, and little playing.

Stephen Dodgson introduced his third piano sonata which was played by Bernard Roberts. Stephen has on several occasions said that it was the encouragement that he received from the Richmond Concert Society that prompted him to write his sonatas for piano, which have all been composed with Bernard Roberts very much in his mind.

I like to think that as members sit down waiting for a concert to start they expect everything to go like clockwork. Hopefully this happens at most concerts, and I would like to think it happened when we put on a gala concert to celebrate our first twenty-five years of concert giving. The actual story behind this concert was quite fraught. The artists taking part were the Allegri

The memorable 25th anniversary concert at the German School. Whilst everyone looks calm before the concert, five minutes after this photograph was taken there was nearly total panic! The Allegri String Quartet together with Valerie Tryon at the piano, the Canadian clarinettist James Campbell on the right, and the author.

String Quartet, the Canadian clarinettist James Campbell, and Valerie Tryon. The programme was to include the great G minor piano quartet of Mozart and the same composer's clarinet quintet. Valerie was going to play some preludes by Rachmaninov in her solo spot, and the whole concert was to be rounded off with all the performers playing together in Prokofiev's delightful *Overture on Hebrew Themes*. The concert was being televised by the Canadian Broadcasting Corporation and the full German School awaited in expectation. Everything was going well, that is until I popped into the room occupied by the performers about ten minutes before the start of the concert. Peter Carter, the leader, was practising to get his fingers into shape, and the same applied to the other members of the quartet and to James Campbell. Valerie was sitting there, calm as always before a concert. All was peace and tranquillity until I made some comment to the quartet's self-appointed librarian, David Roth, about putting the music on the stands which were already on the platform. There was a dreadful silence as he discovered that the quartet's music for the two Mozart works and the Prokofiev had been left in the Wigmore Hall, where they had been playing a day or so before. Without the music there could be no concert. What could one do?

I suppose we could best be described as trying to keep calm whilst panic gently spread among all the players. Then someone had the bright idea to see if any member of the audience happened to have a spare copy of the two Mozart works and the Prokofiev. We could have gone into the audience and asked if anyone had a pound of butter to spare, for all the likelihood of getting any success. As it happened St Cecilia, the patron saint of music, must have been looking down on us. A member of the society, Robin Wade, an amateur cellist, was approached and he said that he had the scores of the Mozart but not the Prokofiev. Robin, bless him, drove to his home on Richmond Hill and got the scores for us, but we still had to deal with the Prokofiev problem. Luckily, Valerie had the score of the Prokofiev which we borrowed from her and photocopied each page, which contained all the parts. Then we made five copies of each page. The concert started about eight minutes late. It was a nightmare beginning to the evening, but as everything turned out the concert was a great success. The audience were treated to two performances of the Prokofiev as the television crew wanted to come on to the platform and film from different angles. The television film is quite a memory of a great evening and has been shown many times on Canadian television. The film also has a short interview with Muriel Dawson, a member of the executive committee at the time, who a few seasons later was to give the society a generous sum of money which allowed us to set up the Muriel Dawson concerts—but more of that later.

Muriel Dawson, whose generosity allowed the society to start a series of concerts for young musicians.

The very next month saw, I think, the smallest audience we have had for a concert for a very long time. It was also one of the most memorable concerts I can recall. The reason for the poor turnout at St Anne's church on Kew Green was the awful weather with blinding snow and ice on the roads. No wonder the audience preferred to stay indoors—that would have been my preference as well. So bad was the weather that it was very difficult to stand upright on the ice, as one's feet slithered in this direction and that. The Hanson String Quartet were playing and it seemed that they were inspired, as I cannot recall such a superb performance of Schubert's *Death and the Maiden* quartet. The Hanson Quartet had enormous potential and we were looking to them to become almost a resident quartet, much in the same way as the Endellion had been. Unfortunately the quartet decided to break up, but not before they gave several more performances for the society in following seasons.

By March the weather had much improved and we welcomed the cellist Steven Isserlis at the German School. Steven plays on gut strings and always with great authority. One remembers the performance of the Shostakovich cello sonata and, something of a curiosity, the dance suite by Mátyás Seiber, who it will be recalled started the Hampton and Teddington Music Club back in the late 1950s. Steven was already a cellist much in demand on the international circuit, and he has had an amazing career ever since.

It is strange how some concerts come about. In the early years of the society, that great pianist John Ogdon came and played for us, and he made a considerable reduction in his fee in order to help the society in its early struggling days. One Sunday morning Monica and I were at St Mary's church in Twickenham for the morning service. There is a moment in the service when you greet people all around you and on this particular Sunday, having greeted Monica and the person on my left, I turned around to welcome the person behind and came face to face with dear John. He was at that time in a halfway house in Strawberry Hill getting over the mental illness which created so much havoc in his career. There he stood looking quite dreadful with cigarette stains all over his dirty jacket. This great bulk of a human being stood there, with his small beard coloured yellow with the stain of tobacco. I was completely taken aback but then John, in his gentle voice said "Hello, Howard" and I responded with "Hello, John." It was really a most touching moment. When the service ended I took John on a short tour of St Mary's showing him the small P marking the place where Alexander Pope was buried in 1744, and also drew his attention to the wall monuments on the north wall of the church commemorating Pope and his parents. Then we went over to the parish room, which at that time, before it was rebuilt, was very small and not very appetising, and we all had a cup of coffee. He was able to bring me up to date and the story he had to tell was a sad story indeed. He had spent some time in a mental hospital for treatment and as a result his career had suffered. In fact John, who had been a pianist everyone wanted to hear, was now a pianist without any engagements.

I decided that I would try to repay him for all the kindness he had shown the society years ago by offering him a recital. He was quite overwhelmed. This recital took place, sponsored by Squire's Garden Centre, on the 19th May 1987. John played a tough programme of Schumann's *Carnaval* and Ravel's *Gaspard de la Nuit* which has that fiendish final section—*Scarbo*—which requires the most secure technique possible. He also played Liszt's *Todtentanz* in the rarely performed solo piano version. John had been diagnosed some little time before as a schizophrenic and the performance was very much like his mental state. There were moments of quite brilliant piano playing where one was very aware of the great intellect of the man shining through; but there were moments especially in the Schumann when the music was pulled around so much that his playing seemed overly sentimental. It proved to be John's last appearance for the society as he sadly died in 1989 at the early age of fifty-two—a great loss to the musical world at large and to his friends.

So this brought the 25th season to a close. It certainly was an eventful one with plenty of excitement but despite all the setbacks and moments of crisis we had kept going.

It was time for some increase in the price of subscription and for the 1987-88 season we increased it to £12.50. The theme of the 26th season was youth and we certainly had plenty of young talent. The intention was to open with a piano recital by Barry Douglas, who had won the Tchaikowsky piano competition in Moscow the previous year, but it was not to be as Barry was taken ill and had to withdraw. I had very little time to find a replacement and this caused much concern for everyone on the committee especially as this was the opening concert of the series, always a critical time for promoters.

When you have a problem it is to your friends that you turn and on this occasion Bernard Roberts came to the rescue and demonstrated yet again what a brilliant pianist he is. Clearly we could not expect Bernard to play the programme which Barry was contracted to play; instead Bernard opened with a Mozart sonata followed by Schubert's *Wanderer* fantasy, and in the second half he performed Schumann's *Kreisleriana*—all pieces which Bernard had under his fingers as he was broadcasting the Schubert and the Schumann within two or three days for Radio 3.

In November we heard an unusual recital by the young and attractive Michala Petri who came with her mother, Hanne. This was a recital of recorder music and it was quite unbelievable what Michala could achieve with her chosen instrument. She was a true virtuoso and although very young when she paid us her first visit, her fame had spread to all the recorder clubs in London, or so it seemed, who crowded into St Margaret's Catholic church.

The Hanson paid another visit to the RCS in February 1986 and on this occasion performed the second of Borodin's two quartets, the Debussy quartet and the Dvorak *American* quartet. They played just once more for the RCS, in 1990 just before they disbanded with all the members of the quartet going their separate ways. It is perhaps understandable that quartets tend to come and go, as the playing together of four minds as if one must place considerable strain on all concerned.

Steven Isserlis made his second appearance in March 1988 and on this occasion the concert was presented in Richmond's Queen Charlotte Hall. Steven as always played impeccably and his programme included the second unaccompanied Bach suite; a Beethoven sonata; the Brahms cello sonata in F major; and a showpiece to bring the recital to a close—the *Hungarian Rhapsody* by Popper, whose works were staple diet for cellists in the years between the wars. As a society we felt that we had to use the Queen Charlotte Hall, which had been largely financed by money provided by the Richmond Parish Lands Charity. It is like a large drill hall and really has little to commend it. I suppose that it must be ranked an improvement on the community centre in Richmond but it has an unfriendly feeling, and it is difficult to put on a serious concert there as noises coming from adjoining rooms can destroy any atmosphere. In this respect it reminded me of the old Richmond community centre.

An interesting concert was given on April 19th 1988 when we invited an excellent string ensemble, known as Opus 20, to play for us at the German School. It was a fascinating programme and one which I felt was very much up their street, as the ensemble specialised in contemporary music. The first half consisted of Andrzej Panufnik's *Arbor Cosmica* which I had heard several times and regarded as one of his most interesting works. He was delighted with the performance the ensemble gave. The other main work was Britten's *Variations on a Theme of Frank Bridge*, a work full of major difficulties of a technical nature for the performers, but which when played well, as happened at this concert, enchants the ear and indeed the mind.

After Angela Hewitt had stepped in at short notice to give the Sidney Harrison memorial concert the previous season, I wanted to engage her again and as at this point in our history we tended to have two piano recitals a season it was a good opportunity to hear her once more. My hope was that she would play Bach's *Goldberg Variations* in view of her special talent to play Bach's keyboard compositions with great clarity and indeed drama, when needed. But it was not to be and I was deeply disappointed. At that time Angela was going through some disturbing personal problems and she felt that she could not undertake a performance of this major piece of music. Instead she played a Beethoven sonata, and the Spanish dances of Granados as well as the waltzes opus 39 by Brahms.

As Barry Douglas had been taken ill just before his scheduled appearance to open the 1987-88 season, he agreed to open the 27th season, which had the unifying theme of Brahms. Barry's recital was rather like the curate's egg. He opened with the six piano pieces of opus 118 by Brahms. I don't know what went wrong but it was generally felt by a number of the members that, as Barry performed them, they made little musical sense. It was all very odd. By the time he arrived at a group of preludes and fugues by Shostakovich he was really back on form and gave them a brilliant reading. For the second half he decided to play the G major piano sonata of Tchaikowsky. I am not convinced that this sonata works, as it relies very much on the skill of the performer to make sense of its sprawling composition. I was well aware of many inadequate performances over the years, but I also realised that a great pianist like Richter could play it and under his fingers it seems a masterpiece. Barry's performance of this elusive piece was quite outstanding and when he came to the end one realised why he had taken Moscow by storm when he won the Tchaikowsky prize.

In October we welcomed for the first time the Vanbrugh String Quartet. They had just won the International String Competition, which in 1988 was based in Portsmouth although a year or so later it moved to London. They played one of the early Beethoven quartets of opus 18 as well as the third Bartok quartet and the Brahms C minor quartet. Although Bartok wrote his quartets in the 1920s and 30s the modern complexity of the music still demands a great deal of concentration on the part of the listener. This is where I try to help by providing a programme note quite devoid, as far as I am able, of musical technical terms but relating to the music as a sound experience, pinpointing certain melodic ideas to grab hold of.

In January 1989 Sarah Walker returned to perform Schubert's *Die Winterreise* with Imogen Cooper. These days it is not that unusual to hear a female voice singing this great and tragic work which is normally performed either by a tenor or baritone voice. Actually I still feel the full impact of this music is better with a male singer, but there was no doubt that Sarah and Imogen gave a deeply committed performance of this towering masterpiece. I remember vividly that after the concert Sarah and Imogen together with members of the committee went back to Dick Gandy's house in Teddington, and over a glass or two of wine Sarah and Dick sang some extracts from Berlioz's opera *The Trojans*, with Imogen battling bravely with the piano part.

Imogen Cooper, a brilliant musical mind combined with a flawless technique, gave a number of recitals for the society.

The Petersen Quartet from East Germany played at St Mary's church in Twickenham and they included the second Brahms opus 51 quartet, which completed the opus 51 set as the Vanbrughs had played the C minor earlier in the season. Richard Harris, in the Richmond and Twickenham Times described the concert as "pure joy" and indeed that just about summed up the general audience reaction to this fine ensemble.

At this time Monica and I left for a number of weeks in Australia, where I was lecturing on credit to the company I had been mainly responsible for setting up many years before. It was a great experience for us both and we loved every moment. Brilliant weather in Melbourne where the first series of lectures took place, and pouring rain in Sydney. Both marvellous cities but possibly because of the weather, Melbourne has a special place in our hearts. As we were away I missed the London Mozart Piano Trio but I gather they gave a most enjoyable recital.

To end the season we had a visit from Hamish Milne. He is yet another under-rated British pianist who has made a speciality of playing the music of Rachmaninov's friend, Nicolai Medtner. On this occasion he played as his main work the *Études Symphoniques* of Schumann and I can say without contradiction that his performance that evening was of a very high standard indeed. Hamish had a bad cold but that did not prevent him playing at the top of his form. Afterwards I received a card from him apologising for his cold and hoping that he had not infected the whole of Richmond!

The decade was drawing to its close. We had decided to retain the subscription at £15, and on paper at least the 1989-90 season looked as if it had plenty to offer.

There were quite a few changes on the political front. Margaret Thatcher had an open quarrel with her chancellor, Nigel Lawson, because she had fallen, in respect of financial philosophy, under the influence of Professor Walters. She fought off a leadership battle, and around the time we started the new season, a new figure emerged as foreign secretary—John Major.

It was also about this time that the Berlin Wall fell, marking symbolically the end of the cold war. So it was a time of new hope as we were about to start a new decade.

Earlier in the year John Ogdon had died so the opening concert given by Martino Tirimo was dedicated to him. Working on the programme with Martino I wanted to include all the first book of preludes by Debussy. We had never programmed these wonderful evocative pictures in music, and Martino was delighted as he had been making a particular study of all Debussy's piano music with the intention of recording his complete piano music. The other main work was Schumann's *Davidsbündlertänze* and this was chosen for two reasons. Firstly Martino is one of the most sensitive pianists that I know and I always felt that he had a particular affinity with Schumann's music. I still recall the performance he gave previously of the *Études Symphoniques*. The other reason was that this particular work was a favourite with Monica so I could hardly resist. The whole recital was a deeply moving one and I am sure the spirit of John would have approved. The theme of the season was Schubert and Debussy, and Martino as well as playing the Debussy preludes also played the little A major sonata by Schubert.

Debussy made another appearance in the October concert when the Petersen Quartet played the only string quartet Debussy had composed. The fact that we had this East German quartet playing so soon after the collapse of the Berlin Wall added a certain poignancy to the evening. A song recital by the young Juliet Booth accompanied by Malcolm Martineau took place in November. Juliet was making quite a name for herself and it was a great pleasure to include her in our new season, especially as she lived on Twickenham Green.

The December concert and the last one of the 1980s was given by Susan Milan, a flautist of quite exceptional talent, and the young Welsh harpist, Caryl Thomas. The combination of flute and harp is ideal in many respects as they have been described as the only musical instruments giving voice without human agency. This might be on the fanciful side but the hollow reed and the plucked strings make a glorious sound.

And so we could look back on the eighties, remembering many moments of great music-making, a few moments of near disaster and moments of genuine sadness as several friends among the committee and the artists we had grown to love passed away. We were only half way through the 1989-90 season but we were all geared up to go into the 1990s with determination to continue giving value for money and the opportunity for our members to hear great music played by fine musicians. Many friendships among members had been forged during the seasons. By October I had retired from the City of London and my underwriting days were over. I needed to face new challenges—some years before at a senior executive lunch I had expressed the view that I would like to retire at the age of sixty and my wish came true. I knew that I would not be bored in retirement as about a year before I had been approached and asked if I would take over the chairmanship of the Richmond upon Thames Arts Council. I gave it a great deal of thought before accepting, but I am glad I did, as I felt the Richmond Arts Council had much to give to the local community. I accepted on the understanding that I could not devote much time, or indeed energy, to the new job until I had shaken off my City responsibilities. Now as I turned my back on the City I entered a new period of my life and with my commitment to the Richmond Concert Society as strong as ever.

Chapter Five

HELPING YOUNG MUSICIANS

For the first five years of the new decade I kept myself busy in retirement by chairing the Richmond upon Thames Arts Council, as well as running the musical side of the Richmond Concert Society. It is perhaps an understatement to say that I was kept busy, as the amount of work involved in running the arts council was greater than I imagined! My involvement with it went way back prior to its actual formation. I was asked by Monty Garrett, who was the mayor in the early 1960s, if I would join the Twickenham steering party to see if it was going to be viable to create a local arts council. A similar steering group had been set up across the river in Richmond and eventually the two steering groups combined to bring into being the Richmond upon Thames Arts Council, once the amalgamation of Twickenham, Barnes and Richmond into one borough had taken place.

The early years of this newly fledged organisation had its problems. There were representatives from a number of the main arts organisations in the area such as the Richmond Shakespeare Society, the Barnes Music Club, and the Richmond Art Society, and I made many good friends. But the problem was that each representative wanted to project their own society rather than take a broad look at the arts in general. The new organisation had some financial support from the then Conservative council but we were in no position to promote any new arts initiative on our own. I recall tortuous hours of writing the constitution with members arguing over the smallest detail. I came to the conclusion that writing or helping to write a constitution was not a gift I had been blessed with and found the whole process frustrating in the extreme.

I mentioned earlier that I made many good friends in this new organisation and I recall names like Vaughan Hoad, who was an early supporter financially of the Richmond Concert Society, and Myrtle Lane, a wonderful woman who for years ran the Barnes Music Club with great success. Myrtle was supportive of me in the early RCS days when our new music society came on to the scene and could have been seen as a rival to the very strong Barnes Music Club. But Myrtle believed passionately in the arts and welcomed our arrival—a gesture which I remember with gratitude. Another good friend was John Oliver, whom I came to know well. John's widow, Jane, was to do sterling work as membership secretary of the Richmond Arts Council during and after my chairmanship.

The very early years of the Richmond Arts Council certainly had their fair share of drama and gradually I came to the conclusion that the council was departing from the ideals we all had at the outset. My City responsibilities were also increasing and I decided that something had to go and therefore tendered my resignation, albeit with some regrets. I am, I suppose, the only surviving member of the original Richmond upon Thames Arts Council and, looking back, I was pleased to rejoin the arts council in 1989 to serve for a period of six years as its chairman. The development of the literary lunch was an event which gave me satisfaction; I worked in very close association with Helena Caletta of the Open Book, an independent bookshop in Richmond, and over the years the lunch increased in stature. We were able to persuade a number of literary luminaries to come and talk after lunch at the Richmond Hill Hotel and among the authors who came were Ludovic Kennedy, Melvyn Bragg, John Mortimer, Elizabeth Jane Howard, Fay Weldon, Victoria Glendinning, and Joanna Trollope. The Richmond Arts Council literary lunch served as the launch pad of Richmond's leisure services "Book Now" festival which under the inspired leadership of Nigel Cutting has put Richmond on the literary map.

Another innovation was the selling of paintings by local artists at the Richmond May fair. I felt that this was a practical way of bringing the talents of many local artists to the forefront, and the May fair was an excellent vehicle. We started out in a very minor way with a small flimsy canopy which blew away in a May gale the following year. I was much indebted to a member of the Arts Council executive, Noel Reynolds, who masterminded the practical ways of setting up this operation. As the years passed the contribution the Richmond Arts Council was to make in the promotion of local artists became a major feature of the annual Richmond May fair.

I have spent some time on my involvement with the Richmond Arts Council for several reasons. It has become a major part of the borough's arts activities; its early history, to the best of my knowledge, has never been recorded before and needs to be stated; and also I received great satisfaction in being its chairman for a period of six years. On personal grounds it made a perfect bridge from a long career in the City to one of more sustained retirement.

On the political front Margaret Thatcher ceased to be the prime minister in 1990 and John Major succeeded her. The problem that divided the Conservative Party then, and continued throughout John Major's premiership, was our role in Europe. As it turned out the Richmond Concert Society turned its eye towards Europe as a number of European musicians were welcome participants at our concerts. It was just the way things developed, as we continued our search for musical excellence in order to put concerts of an international standard before the very discriminating Richmond Concert Society audience.

That season we had decided to redesign the brochure and programme covers and after much research we picked on a picture, the original of which is kept in the Orleans Gallery—*Richmond from beneath the Railway Bridge* attributed to the artist George Hilditch who was born in 1803 and died in 1857. It was in many ways an ideal picture to decide upon as it has the railway bridge arch to provide a frame for both the brochure and the programme cover. We kept it for quite a few seasons and it did excellent service. It is featured on the cover of this book.

Having left the 1980s with the sound of a flute and harp singing in our ears— and many members still recall the playing of Susan Milan and Caryl Thomas with much pleasure—we celebrated the start of the nineties with a large undertaking—a full symphony orchestra. Well, it was not quite the London Symphony or the London Philharmonic, but the Richmond upon Thames Youth Orchestra. I have always been fascinated by arranging concerts with large numbers, and I can still see in my mind's eye the terror on the faces of the executive committee. Yes, of course it requires the most intensive planning and we always have the problem of venue. Possibly an orchestra of nearly eighty players could fit into the German School but there would not be much room left for the poor audience. I say this with some feeling as I actually did put the Richmond Youth Orchestra into that venue, and, yes, there really was not much room left for the audience, but that was not for an audience of the size of the RCS.

So we had to look further afield and our eyes lighted upon St Edmund's Catholic church in Whitton. It is a good venue and for a large gathering of players has a reasonable acoustic. It also has the space as well by using the chancel area. But we did run into problems which at times looked as if they were going to be impossible to solve. Shortly before we arranged the concert as part of the 1989-90 season the Pope had decreed that Roman Catholic churches were not to be used for secular music. This rule had never worried Father Desmond Swan of St Margaret's Catholic church but it did concern the fathers of St Edmund's to some extent although they were quite realistic. It was the church lay members who saw the problems and mounted some opposition. I remember trying to persuade them that the performance of strictly classical music glorified the Holy Spirit, and gradually one by one they came round and the concert went ahead with all the co-operation one could ask from the clergy of the church.

As chairman of the Richmond upon Thames Arts Council I also had as one of my responsibilities the running of the youth orchestra. I found it a much more difficult role than negotiating with professional artists. I needed to argue a case before the separate committee which ran the orchestra and I put forward a scheme whereby the Richmond Concert Society would bear the cost of hiring the venue and the cost of engaging a professional soloist. The youth orchestra would bear all other costs. In other words they would take the profit from any tickets sold on the door whilst the society took responsibility for the general organisation of the event. It was a fair compromise and the concert worked well.

The conductor was Jonathan Butcher and it was left to me to decide on the soloist in the Brahms violin concerto. I decided to invite Krzystof Smietana, a brilliant violinist who had already given a recital for the RCS which had left a strong impression.

The quality of the playing was really quite extraordinary. Here was a large group of young people drawn from state schools in the borough and independent schools tackling fine pieces from the orchestral repertoire such as the *Symphonic Variations* of Dvorak and the Brahms violin concerto and making an excellent sound. The concert opened with an overture by Elizabeth Lutyens. It drew a capacity audience made up of members and, of course, the parents of the children taking part. It was a gamble which worked.

Later the arts council ran into problems with the youth orchestra, which only met during the school holidays and eventually ceased to operate in this way. Mainly the problem was getting co-operation with some borough employees and it became clear that the whole concept of mixing independent schools and borough schools together was not viewed with much favour by the Richmond council—don't ask me why. Later the council started the Music Trust to run music teaching in the borough schools and I was asked if I would be a trustee of this new organisation which I accepted and this has run well for the past few years.

One of the violinists in the youth orchestra was the young Laura Samuels and she went on to study at the Royal College of Music and became the second violin in the brilliant Belcea String Quartet who have performed for the RCS on a number of occasions, in the late nineties and in the 2000-2001 season.

The concerts between January and May 1990 were of a high standard. The outstanding recorder player Michala Petri came over from Holland and gave a recital with her mother Hanne in St Mary's church in Twickenham. This was the second time that Michala had visited us and one could only wonder afresh at her sheer virtuosity on the recorder. Just about every recorder player in outlying boroughs turned up to hear her and although the church was full for the concert it seemed that members in general gave it a miss, obviously thinking that an evening listening to the sound of a recorder was not to their taste. They missed a great concert.

The Hanson String Quartet returned to play for us, performing an early Mozart quartet, Bartok's fourth quartet and Beethoven's opus 127. Every time I heard the Hanson I was impressed and really I wanted them as a sort of adopted quartet for the society, but it was not to be as later the four of them decided to go their separate ways.

The season ended with a Schubert piano recital by Imogen Cooper, who during this period had concentrated on this composer's piano music and had made a number of highly impressive recordings of the sonatas. Imogen is a highly cultivated musician and her recital was outstanding in many ways and it brought the season to a very satisfactory close.

The new season had an international flavour about it. We had artists from Russia, Austria, France, Italy and Japan. It all looked very impressive and by and large the season worked well.

It started out with a piano quartet known as the Villiers, who had played for us a few seasons before, and they performed the two delightful piano quartets by Dvorak; in between these works we introduced something of a novelty, Martinu's three madrigals for two violins. The pianist was the ever reliable Ian Brown known as the mainstay of the international Nash Ensemble, who were going to appear a number of years later at the end of the decade.

From Russia we had a pianist of great sensitivity in Mikhail Rudy. Actually, Mikhail had left Russia some years before and had then settled in Paris. He put up with the Parisian music scene for a few years but I got the impression that he found it very oppressive and then decided to leave France and make his home in London. He gave an impressive performance of Ravel's *Gaspard de la Nuit* and the technical nightmare of the final piece *Scarbo* held no terrors for him at all. Whilst his career became more established one has the impression that the London music scene has tended to ignore him apart from the odd Royal Festival Hall concert.

The Austrian contingent was the Haydn Trio of Vienna. This group are old friends of the society and I believe that the pianist, Heinz Medjimorec, was godfather to Paul Bowen's son. Paul has been for many years one of the cornerstones of the Richmond Concert Society as treasurer and as the person whose computer layout skills make sure that the concert programmes are set up and printed.

The Haydn Trio of Vienna played only two works in their programme, but what works! The *Archduke* trio of Beethoven is a monumental piece, not necessarily in size but in musical content. The second half was devoted to the A minor piano trio of Tchaikowsky. The piece made many friends that evening and I was determined to bring it back some seasons later.

In February 1991 we had a recital by a young violinist from the Yehudi Menuhin School, Daniel Hope. He showed even in his early teens an amazing technique and musicality. As I write in 2002 Daniel is very much on the international circuit and building an impressive career. So we spotted a talent early and can bask to a small extent in his glory.

In March things all went wrong. It does happen every now and again and when it does happen naturally one goes through anxious moments. I had heard the Italian cellist Arturo Bonucci at the Bishopsgate Institute and found him to be a virtuoso of great technical ability and musical sensitivity. Then a few days before the recital Arturo crushed his hand in a car door, and that to a large degree brought his career to a tragic end. What does one do when this happens? Simply seek another artist who is capable of giving a programme at short notice, and this is what I did. Moray Welsh, one of this country's leading cellists, stepped into the breach and gave a recital of quality. I can assure you I was most relieved.

We ended the season with a piano recital. Where possible we like to have such a recital because for many years the established sponsor for the final concert of the season has been Squire's Garden Centre and Colin Squire has a passion for the piano. He tells me that he has been delighted with the many famous pianists who have performed at the last event. On this occasion I had invited the young and attractive Japanese pianist Noriko Ogawa. Noriko has built up a formidable career and she is a very fine pianist. If the concert did not live up to my full expectations I have only one person to blame—myself. The reason is simple. I had it in my mind that the second half of the recital should be devoted to a performance of the four Chopin ballades. Now, Norika had in her repertoire two of these well known works and, generous soul that she was, learned the other two especially for the Richmond recital. I thought it would work hearing the four ballades as a set, but Chopin never intended them to be played together and although they can be heard in this way in the Wigmore Hall or the Queen Elizabeth Hall they are such great pieces that to hear them one after the other in a strange way diminishes the individual works. It is not the same problem with the twenty-four preludes of Chopin which work wonderfully one after the other.

I hope that at the end of the season the members of the society felt that they had had their money's worth as we had made a small increase in the subscription for the season to £18.

Any new season takes months to organise because it is not always possible to get the artists you wish to have when you want them, as they might well be out of the country on tour. We have to make sure that the balance of the concerts is right and that we do not have two piano recitals one after the other, or string quartets for that matter. For the purpose of balance we need to have a song recital midway through the season. It is a strange fact that song recitals used to be the least attended of all our concerts and why this should be is a mystery. What I do know is that the majority of concert societies have long since stopped putting on vocal concerts and this is a shame, but I can understand it, because if the audience is small one does get a bit disheartened! I know of one concert society who spent a great deal of money on the well known *Songmaker's Almanac* with Graham Johnson at the piano and singers of the ilk of Felicity Lott and Ann Murray. The audience fell to under fifty and they lost a great deal of money. Put the *Songmaker's Almanac* on at the Wigmore Hall and you have to beg to get tickets.

At the RCS we have consistently put on a vocal recital each season and whilst I admit that audiences many seasons ago were poor we persisted, and I am glad to say that these days audiences for song recitals are as good as for any other type of concert. It just takes time and patience to demonstrate to an audience that buried in the vast amount of German lied, French chanson and English song are great works of art. On the subject of song recitals I have always felt that the audience are entitled to know, for example, what German songs are all about, so we have always done our best to provide full English translations in order to enhance the listener's enjoyment. Most singers these days have a career in the opera house and the odd engagement giving song recitals. The money is to be made in the opera house and certainly not on the recital stage but the buzz singers get in meeting the demands of the concert platform is felt to be worth the fee cut they have to sustain.

Most singers love to include Hugo Wolf in their programmes, and I can understand why this should be. Wolf had a genius for setting words to music possibly better than any other composer, Schubert included. He is a most satisfactory composer to perform whether you are a singer or a pianist yet the musical public, in the main, still find him difficult to accept. This is a pity as the songs in the *Italian Songbook*, for example, are quite exquisite.

The 1991-92 season followed the broad outline of previous seasons but there was the introduction of a new type of concert which I will touch upon later. The new season started with a string quartet concert given by the well known Allegri String Quartet who played a Haydn quartet, the Schubert A minor quartet and the ever popular Ravel quartet. On this occasion (unlike in 1986) they brought their music with them.

The next concert used period instruments and it was given by the Beethoven Broadwood Piano Trio. It was an interesting event as the piano used was an original square piano of a period possibly a few years later than Beethoven but nevertheless with a most distinctive sound. The performances were of a high standard and the concert was much enjoyed.

In December I suppose I went over the top, much to the irritation of my fellow committee members. I do this from time to time and hope that they will forgive me! On this occasion I persuaded the executive committee that it would be interesting to put on a concert at the Normansfield Theatre which lies between Teddington and Hampton Wick on the road to Kingston. This unique theatre is in the grounds of what was then a home for a number of people suffering from the chromosome disorder known as Down's syndrome, which was named after Dr John Langdon Down who did the research into this disorder. It was opened in 1868 as a private training home where residents with these mental disabilities were taken in and treated very much as members of the family.

Langdon Down must have been an extraordinary and deep thinking man because he felt that his "residents" would respond to entertainment in the theatre he built as part of the large hospital. Indeed Langdon Down insisted that all his staff should be capable of entertaining the residents either by singing or playing a musical instrument.

I had the opportunity of going round the theatre and was quite enchanted. Here was a true Victorian theatre in our own borough and nobody knew much about it and certainly very few, if any, of the members would have seen it. The backstage is a mass of small rooms and passageways and on stage you could see the slots where scenery was fixed, and there were also old back-cloths such as the only surviving part of the original set for the Savoy Theatre's premiere of Gilbert and Sullivan's *Ruddigore*. It was all very exciting and I wanted desperately to put on a concert there just to see what the acoustics were like. I suspected that they would be good but was taken back a bit by how good they actually were.

There were problems. Fire regulations dictated that only about one hundred and fifty seats could be put in the theatre. To tell the truth the number should have been far fewer but somehow this got forgotten in all the fun and games in putting this event on. We limited the number of members who could come to one hundred and fifty and they had to make special application for tickets. They went, as expected, very quickly.

But we had nothing to sit down on and this is where our sponsor that evening was so wonderful. Reed Exhibition Companies Limited in Richmond understood exactly what we were setting out to do. They spoke to one of their customers and they delivered and collected the next day the required number of chairs at no cost, and I thought this was a wonderful and most generous gesture. Lord Rix and his wife, the actress Elspet Gray, who were devoted to the Normansfield Hospital came to the concert as this was the first time a musical event had been held in the theatre in living memory.

The artists were the London Oboe Quartet and they performed an interesting programme including Britten's *Phantasy* quartet for oboe and strings and Mozart's delightful oboe quartet. The evening was a triumph, but I learned that delightful as the theatre was it was not large enough to present on a viable basis concerts of the high standard we sought. It had, certainly at that time, the advantage of easy parking but so much money needed to be expended on the theatre to satisfy the licensing authorities that for public performances it could not pay its way.

I remember the rehearsal on the afternoon of the concert. Sitting there listening to the music were a number of the remaining residents and they clearly loved every moment. I could not help feeling that Dr Langdon Down would have been pleased.

A new type of concert was introduced in February 1992 and it came about in this way. For a number of years a loyal member of the committee of the RCS was Muriel Dawson. She was a diminutive figure and although she was Welsh by birth she had lost her accent. She lived in a lovely flat on Church Road in Richmond and had made her career in the civil service. Muriel had been awarded the MBE, of which she was very proud. She had by repute a good soprano voice although by the time I got to know her she had given up singing altogether. To the arts in Richmond Muriel was very generous and had given a donation to the Richmond upon Thames Arts Council to run a poetry competition for young children.

She wanted to use what money she had to benefit others and although towards the end of her life Muriel was somewhat eccentric, all those who came into contact with her warmed to her personality. I know that as she got older she seemed to be concerned how best to dispose of her money and sought advice from many of her friends.

She spoke to me and wondered if the Richmond Concert Society could organise each year a competition for singers or instrumentalists and said that if this was possible then it would give her pleasure to provide a sum of money. Really the idea, which possibly sprang into her mind as a result of the successful Leeds International Piano Competition, was not a practical one from our point of view. I thought for some time about how I could respond to her and then put forward a scheme whereby each season we would present a concert for young musicians who were at the end of their training and about to embark on one of the most critical stages in a difficult career—the moment when they needed as much exposure as possible.

The idea attracted Muriel and she presented the society with a cheque for £3,000 in order to fund this type of event. We decided that we would call the concert the Muriel Dawson concert and so it has remained to the present day. The first concert consisted of a young baritone and a piano trio. It was most successful and the piano trio, in particular, made a good impression. Muriel was at the concert and enjoyed it a lot, although I suspected that she would have preferred to have remained anonymous. The name of the piano trio on that occasion was the Gould. Since we gave them this opportunity to perform in front of an attentive audience they have gone on to become one of this country's leading piano trios and indeed in the 1998-99 season they returned to St Margaret's Catholic church, the scene of their earlier success, as an established international piano trio.

Muriel only lived to attend two of her concerts but when she died I was asked by her family if I would say a few words at her funeral, which I felt honoured to do. So every season Muriel is remembered with affection by all who knew her. Her sister Dorothy also gave a most generous donation to the society to go towards the initial funding provided by Muriel. The money remains untouched as capital and we try to finance the concerts out of interest earned on the capital but, as in the intervening years interest rates have tended to be on the low side, it has been necessary to subsidize the mounting costs of presenting the Muriel Dawson concerts.

The following month we presented a concert at St Mary's church in Hampton by a young quartet, the Kreutzer. They performed in memory of our much loved president, Andrzej Panufnik, who had died in October 1991; they played his third string quartet, which he had composed in 1990 and had titled *Wycinanki*. This name came about from Andrzej's "lifelong attachment to the rustic art of Poland, especially the paper cuts (*wycinanki* in Polish), symmetrical designs of magical abstract beauty and rustic charm"— Andrzej's words not mine. It was written as the test piece of the 1991 London International String Quartet Competition and was given its official first performance by the quartet which won the competition that year—the Wihan. Little did I know that a number of years later the Wihan Quartet would perform for us with great success. As a tribute to Andrzej, local poet Brian Louis Pearce had composed a poem called *Glover's Ait* especially for this concert, and this he recited at the start. The programme included Bartok's impressive third quartet as well as one of Beethoven's *Rasumovsky* quartets.

Andrzej had been our president since the 1969 season and had always been most supportive of what we were trying to achieve. It was the unanimous decision of the executive that we should ask Camilla, Andrzej's widow, to take on the role of president, which she kindly agreed to do.

The final concert of the 1991-92 season was a piano recital by Peter Katin playing repertoire clearly very close to his heart, such as four Schubert impromptus and Chopin's third piano sonata in B minor. And so another season drew to its close and based on the views of many members it had been another successful and rewarding one.

There is always a buzz of excitement when a new season starts. After months of negotiation with all its frustrations and thrills everything should be in place to start off yet again on another voyage of discovery, as we put before the members a

Lady Panufnik, our president since 1991, and a constant supporter of the society.

programme of new as well as established repertoire. At the last annual general meeting Richard Gandy indicated his desire to retire as chairman and John Ould was elected to take his place. A change of chairman is quite a moment in a society's history but little did anyone of the established executive committee realize the magnitude of the change, as since the setting up process of the society back in the 1960s, we had had only two chairmen. John in fact had only served as a normal member of the executive during the 1991-92 season before being elected into the position of chairman, but what a success he has been.

John proved from the outset that he had a genius for always finding the right word for the right occasion. His introductions to the concerts are little concise gems, always to the point and bursting with a quiet but effective wit. Committee meetings are a meeting together of friends and not, as sometimes happens, an arena of confrontation and this is thanks to John's fine leadership. He was an accountant and he served with distinction as financial director of The Wallpaper Manufacturers Limited, a major industrial company in the Reed Group. He was able to bring to the society his accountancy skills which, as the years progressed, became even more vital, as the charity commissioners tightened up the rules and regulations which determine the workings of charities.

John is a man of many talents and interests. He has expressed an interest in bell-ringing, brass-rubbing, poetry (he is exceedingly well read),

To set the mood of a concert John Ould's charming and witty introductions are a delight.

and beer. The society was so fortunate to have John and he, more than anyone else, has cemented the executive committee together, which is no mean feat when you consider the various personalities involved.

The season opened with what I regarded as a most sensitive piano recital. It was given by the young French virtuoso, Bernard d'Ascoli. The remarkable thing about Bernard was the attention he gave to the composer's instructions down to the minutest detail. Yet Bernard was blind, so this ability to honour the composer's wishes could only be done by resorting to Braille. He played the charming *Valses Nobles et Sentimentales* of Ravel and a selection from the second book of preludes by Debussy. Apart from a Chopin group the other main work was Schubert's great C minor sonata. Of the last three sonatas that Schubert wrote at the end of his short life the C minor sonata is the least heard—that is, by every other society than the RCS. We have programmed it at least four times, almost it seems to the detriment of the A major and B flat major sonatas. No matter, it is a great piece of music and the last movement seems, looking at the score, to go on for ever. However, Schubert writes with so much variety and drama that this particular movement flashes by in a short and absorbing period of time.

The Budapest String Quartet played for us in November of 1992 and included in their programme a Bartok quartet, the fifth, and Schubert's *Death and the Maiden* quartet. Both received respectable performances. Stanley Grundy was the sponsor for this concert and it became quite clear to me that Stanley and Bartok did not mix. I have made sure that when I invite him to come to a concert or indeed to sponsor one, which he has generously done for many years, I will not subject him to the dissonances of Bela Bartok.

We had a near disaster at the December concert and I know that John Ould, as chairman, was taken aback. We had engaged the brilliant Raphael Ensemble and we decided to mount this event in St Matthias' church in Richmond. This building serves as a church on Sundays and as a community centre for the rest of the week. Whilst the acoustic is all right it is not ideal and there was, certainly when we held this particular concert, quite a buzz coming from the central heating system. But the disaster nearly happened at the start of the concert. John had given his few words of welcome and we all clapped the artists. Of the five instrumentalists the leader, Anthony Marwood, one of this country's finest violinists both as a soloist and as a chamber music player, came on last. He slipped on the step as he mounted the platform and very nearly put his hand through his priceless violin. John did everything to pacify him as he left the platform and Anthony told me years later that he recalls bursting into laughter and could not stop. This was the way the shock took him. We eventually started some minutes later and the whole ensemble played beautifully, opening as they did with that exquisite prelude to the opera *Capriccio* by Richard Strauss, which is concerned with who plays the dominant role in writing an opera—the composer or the poet. The rest of the programme was by Brahms—one of his rarely performed string quintets and the B flat sextet, whose slow movement must be one of the most moving pieces he ever composed.

The January 1993 concert was intended to contain a tour de force. It was to be a performance of a very short one-act opera for solo voice by Judith Weir. The singer who was engaged to perform this quite remarkable work was Eileen Hulse, a young singer supported by the Young Concert Artists Trust, an organisation which we have worked closely with for some years. It was not to be. Recitals are planned many months in advance of the actual concert date—we have to work this way in order to make sure we engage the artists we want and to have everything ready to produce a brochure. In between contracting with Eileen and the concert date, Eileen became pregnant and actually had the baby, if I recall correctly, about the time she was supposed to have performed. We wished her all the best and started to search for a replacement.

Ann Mackay agreed to do the recital for us with the original accompanist, Paul Turner. Clearly we could not expect Ann to sing the same programme but she certainly went out of her way to design a programme to reflect the fact that this was the first time we had a president's concert. She included in her programme Andrzej Panufnik's lovely *Hommage à Chopin* as well as *She Walks in Beauty,* a poem by Lord Byron set to music by Andrzej and Camilla Panufnik's highly talented daughter Roxanna. Ann Mackay looked beautiful as she walked on to the platform and won many hearts that evening. It was a recital with a far ranging programme starting with Alessandro Scarlatti and taking in Mozart, Richard Strauss, Hahn, Britten and William Walton along the way.

Another concert I recall vividly that season was the one given by the well known Gabrieli String Quartet. It was the first visit of this distinguished quartet to the RCS. At that time the Gabrielis were having some problems as they had lost their long time leader, Kenneth Sillito, and as a result the quartet were somewhat rudderless. Then they engaged a young Belgian violinist, Konstantine Stoianov, whom I knew well as he lived in Richmond. I was fairly well informed about Konstantine's day to day emotional turmoils. By this time he and his German wife had divorced and he had become the leader of the London Philharmonic Orchestra. Certainly Konstantine had an amazing talent. Yehudi Menuhin held him in high regard and described him as "one of the most excellent violinists I know". He made a brilliant leader of the Gabrieli and fitted in well with the long established team of Brendan O'Reilly, playing second violin, Ian Jewel, who had performed in the Normansfield concert, playing the viola, and Keith Harvey, a cellist of legendary repute. The concert of Haydn, Janacek and Dvorak has remained long in my memory.

In May 1993 a piano recital by an old friend and patron of the society, Martino Tirimo, brought the season to a close with performances of Schumann's *Kreisleriana* and Schubert's last sonata in B flat. We could look back on a season which had its highlights and contained, which is only natural, other performances which were not quite up to the standard we were always striving to reach.

We had increased the subscription for that season to £20 and we maintained it for the following season. Setting the level of subscription is never really a problem. In the very early days of the society we were under increasing pressure from the National Federation of Music Societies to make a substantial increase and this we had resisted strongly as we always wanted our concerts to be affordable by all. We certainly did not wish the Richmond Concert Society to be seen as elitist and open only to those who could afford the subscription. Looking back I am sure that the stand we took in the 1960s and 1970s, although it cost us dearly in terms of funding denied, was the right one. I say this because those societies and music clubs all over the country who followed the advice of the funding bodies suffered much from declining membership and audiences and many ceased to function. This is a sad fact as the concert societies which were started after the last war provided much needed income and encouragement for musicians. We have been able to keep our subscription down, despite rising costs, because everyone connected with the running of the Richmond Concert Society gives freely of their time and no one is paid a penny for the services that they give. We are therefore one of the few remaining organisations, certainly in the Richmond upon Thames borough, who can be described as truly voluntary—which made our constant requests for money to the borough's voluntary grants committee perfectly reasonable and all the more frustrating when year after year we were refused even a penny's grant.

We exist to present a series of concerts of a high professional standard at a level of subscription which gives good value for money, and I have never heard any complaint that we charge too much.

I believe it is our function to present as balanced a series of concerts as budgets permit. One of the points raised from time to time is the apparent absence of wind concerts. I think there is some validity in this, although we have put on over the years a number of concerts which come into this category. The problem is one of repertoire but I believe we found a good solution when we opened the 1993-94 season with a visit from one of the best wind ensembles around at that time—the Haffner, directed by Nicholas Daniel, a one time winner of the BBC Young Musician competition. Their programme included those delicious wind pieces, the octet partita in F major by Krommer and Hummel's E flat wind partita. These pieces are not very well known but they both have such a lift that all one's cares fade away when the music starts. The E flat major wind serenade by Mozart occupied most of the second half. For myself I love the sound of wind instruments interplaying with each other, but it does tend to displease some of the audience.

The Gaudier Ensemble is made up of leading instrumentalists from this country and Europe. Their concerts are always well worth hearing.

A group who provide music of the highest merit is the Gaudier Ensemble and here we had more wind involved plus strings. The Gaudier Ensemble give each year a festival lasting a few days in the small town of Cerne Abbas in Dorset. Their concert for us included two works which we had not previously programmed. The Beethoven sextet for two horns and strings and the Spohr octet, a piece which I only knew slightly, worked very well together. A glorious performance of the Brahms clarinet quintet took up the second half of the programme and every time I hear this piece I grow to love it more. Brahms wrote it at the end of his life, indeed after he had decided to retire from composing but was encouraged to start again on hearing the clarinet playing of Richard Mühlfeld.

We had two string quartets that season—a return visit from the Budapest playing Beethoven (opus 18 No 6), the second quartet by Kodaly and Schubert's well known A minor quartet; and the Vellinger, one of the most outstanding quartets, in my opinion, that we have engaged. They played the Mendelssohn F minor quartet and I recall finding a seat in a crowded St Mary's church in Twickenham at the rear of the gallery and being somewhat surprised at the quality of the acoustic of this church especially for quartet music. The Mendelssohn F minor quartet made, I think, a strong impression on everyone who heard it. This quartet is not the light-fingered piece which characterises so much of Mendelssohn's output. It is full of music of great poignancy, written as it was soon after the death of his deeply loved sister, Fanny. The two other works also made a deep impression—the first quartet of Janacek and the Elgar quartet. The Janacek was receiving its first hearing at a Richmond Concert Society event. Elgar's E minor string quartet, like his piano quintet, was written late in life and it belongs to the same period as the cello concerto. I recall mentioning in the programme notes how Monica and I had sought out the small cottage in Sussex, known as Brinkwells, where all these works had been composed.

The Australian pianist Piers Lane gave the second of the two piano recitals that season. Piers is one of those delightful men, very friendly and a super pianist. He seems to have no problem performing the most taxing works in the piano repertoire. On this occasion he played all the Schumann opus 12 *Fantasiestücke* and the twelve studies opus 25 by Chopin. The technical and musical problems these studies present are gigantic yet Piers, at the end of such a tough programme, seemed as fresh as ever.

The year 1994 was the year that Mandela became president of South Africa. It was also the year that saw the death of John Smith, the leader of the Labour Party, and the election, totally unopposed, of Tony Blair as leader. Even in 1994 the press were forecasting that in the not too distant future he would become the next prime minister. This was not too difficult a forecast to make as the Conservative government was split so much on the question of Europe. With such a small majority in the House of Commons the prime minister of the day, John Major, was finding it almost impossible to govern.

We had put together, I think, an attractive programme to present to the membership of the society. I remember telling the executive committee year after year that we could not take for granted the loyalty of the members of the RCS. They deserved the best we could offer them but we had to market each season as if it was our first. I suppose this philosophy dates back to the critical early years of the society when I remember going round on a bicycle imploring members to rejoin just in order to keep the society going. It seems a long time ago now and I suppose my gloomy remarks to my fellow committee members were intended to say, now that membership was strong and had been so for several years past, that we must never be complacent.

We started with a wind concert in order to pacify a number of members who felt that we had ignored this type of concert. It was not, I felt, a success because however good the performers might be the range of repertoire is slight in content. True, there are masterworks like the Nielsen quintet, which was performed, but I must admit that I found one of Hindemith's *Kammermusik* tedious.

For a few years the record industry in this country, and indeed abroad, had to contend with a new cheap label, Naxos, and whilst their records were originally distributed through Woolworth's, gradually major stores such as HMV and Tower started stocking their titles. They have now become a major force in the CD market and I think with justification as they cover a very extensive repertoire not always obtainable from the traditional labels. One of Naxos's earliest projects was to record all the Haydn quartets, and there are over eighty of them. All the quartets were to be recorded by the Kodály Quartet from Budapest. When they started to appear they received rave reviews from the critics, which were well deserved. We decided that we would try to get in touch with the Kodály Quartet and invite them to Twickenham to give a concert at St Mary's church. They came in October 1994 and played the Haydn *Lark* quartet, the Ravel quartet and a Brahms, his opus 51 No 1. They lived up to all our expectations and I found them, despite their halting English, easy to work with.

In the very early days of the society we had invited an outstanding young pianist, Anthony Goldstone, to give a recital. Tony Goldstone has never relied on agents to get him work and he does it all himself and was never bashful about writing or ringing me up. I have always had the highest regard for his pianistic qualities and regard him and his delightful wife, Caroline Clemmow, as friends. I heard them give a recital of four hands on one piano and was quite taken aback by their performance. Tony had got hold of a very rare copy of Rimsky-Korsakov's own arrangement for four hands of his orchestral masterpiece *Scheherazade* and it was quite staggering how the vivid orchestral colours were transcribed to the piano. It has to be heard to be believed and I wanted the members of the RCS to hear them perform it. They came in November and played it to great acclaim. It was

ANTHONY GOLDSTONE & CAROLINE CLEMMOW

Anthony Goldstone and his wife Caroline Clemmow pictured on the author's signed CD insert. They are brilliant piano duettists, and performed Rimsky-Korsakov's own transcription of Scheherazade *to great acclaim.*

preceded by Stravinsky's own arrangement of his ballet *Petruschka* and this was also impressive.

Although we do everything possible to keep our concerts on Tuesdays there are occasions when this cannot happen because of contractual commitments the artists have elsewhere. This happened at the start of December 1994 when the Haydn Trio of Vienna paid us another visit, having conducted a master-class at the Royal Academy of Music on the Tuesday evening. It was memorable for a performance they gave of the Smetana piano trio, a work of great charm and beauty.

There is a wide gap between a recorded performance on CD, which might well have received extensive editing, and a live performance. There is, in my opinion, no contest between the two types of performance. The live performance might well have a few minor blemishes such as the odd wrong note or somewhat poor balance. My reaction is "So what?" The live performance is capable of making the hair curl and the adrenaline flow. This sometimes happens, although rarely, on the recorded performance which, as I have said, can be subject to extensive editing. I recall a conversation I had with Valerie Tryon about her highly acclaimed recording of the Chopin ballades and scherzi. I was much taken with her performance of the fourth ballade and listening to it I found myself literally sitting on the edge of my seat. I think she told me the reason. She did the recording at one sitting and without any editing. It was a performance of great poetry and sensitivity and naturally amazing technical brilliance. In other words it was in essence a live performance captured on tape. I had my reservations about the quality of the sound on this recording but that is another matter.

The Haydn Trio of Vienna are able to infuse technical brilliance with sensitive phrasing into their live performance and that is one reason why they are always very welcome at our concerts.

When Eileen Hulse had to call off her earlier appearance on account of her pregnancy I asked her to get in touch with me when things had settled down and she felt fit to resume her concert career. This is what she did, and we gave her a warm welcome in January 1995. The highlight was to be Judith Weir's *King Harald's Saga* and if ever there was a virtuoso work for a singer then this was it. Judith Weir set herself the task of writing a three-act opera for eight solo roles, as well as a part for the Norwegian army. In itself this was quite a feat, but if it involved only one soprano voice singing all eight roles (and not forgetting at least a part of the Norwegian army) without the support of a piano, then one could only sit back and be staggered at the result. The story concerns the invasion of England by the Norwegian King Harald and how he met defeat at the Battle of Stamford Bridge in 1066 just a few weeks before the English king, Harold, marched his army to the south to meet the other better known invasion by William the Conqueror.

So here was Eileen Hulse involving herself in singing arias, a duet with herself as Harald alternating as one of his wives, as well as singing the chorus representing the Norwegian army. It was brilliantly done but what the audience actually thought about it I am not quite sure! I do know that when Eileen left the platform to recover, members of the audience flocked around the music stand which was still holding the vocal score.

Later in the season we invited the Gabrieli String Quartet to play for us once again; by then they had had a further change of personnel in that Konstantine Stoianov had left the quartet to become the concertmaster (really the leader of the orchestra) of the Metropolitan Opera in New York, one of the top positions in the music business. His place was taken by the violinist Yossi Zivoni who had in the not too distant past given a recital for us with Valerie Tryon. Whilst Yossi was a brilliant violinist, of that there was no doubt, he lacked charisma as a soloist but seemed more at home as leader of a quartet. Certainly he settled in well and has remained with the quartet. We decided that we would associate ourselves with the 50th anniversary of the founding of the United Nations and therefore this quality concert was dedicated to the work of the United Nations, and the society was host to the local association.

Because I was on holiday in the Holy Land with Monica, I had to miss the piano recital by Anya Alexeyev, which was a great pity because I heard that she made a very good impression on all those who heard her. I know Anya to be highly gifted so it came as no surprise to me that she went down well and I would love to have heard her performance of a number of the pieces from the Italian book of Liszt's *Années de Pèlerinage*. This was one of two or three concerts I have missed over a forty year period. The concert was masterminded by the chairman, John Ould, who did everything to make sure that Anya was made as comfortable as possible between trying out the Steinway piano and the concert itself—this extended to John and Betty, his wife, taking Anya home with them so that she could have a sleep in their spare bedroom before having tea.

A group known as Hausmusik performed for us in May and whilst they had made one or two highly successful CD recordings on period instruments I found this a most disappointing concert mainly because I am not that keen on the sound of original instruments despite the current vogue for authenticity. The concert did highlight one difference between listening to a CD, with all the advantages of editing and balance, and a live performance. Here, with the players on the stage of the German School, it seemed to me that they took an age after each movement of the Beethoven E flat major septet and the Schubert octet to retune. In the case of the Schubert work with its several movements the performance seemed to go on for ever.

The first concert of any season is quite clearly an important one. It stands a good chance of attracting a large audience and so hopefully everything will go right. On the 26th September 1995, the first concert of the 34th season, as far as I was concerned everything went wrong.

We had decided to make the concert a memorial one to a good friend of the RCS, Isador Caplan. It was Isador who years before suggested that we make application to the reconstituted Richmond Parish Lands Charity. Isador's wife, Joan, was a long-term member of the executive committee in the early years, so it seemed very appropriate that we should honour the memory of a man who had been supportive to us in the past. He had attended the Hausmusik concert of the previous season, although very frail, and members who knew him made a great fuss of him. I believe that gave him a great deal of pleasure. Actually it was quite a feat to get him to the German School as he made it quite clear that he disliked the idea of a German school so close to where he lived in Petersham. It must have been a reaction to the horrors of the last war and what the Nazis did to the Jewish population.

Between the two concerts Isador died and I discussed with his daughter, Sally Simon, the possibility of a memorial concert for him. She drew up a list of friends she would like to invite, and the effect of the numbers of members who usually turn up plus the guest list provided John Ould with possibly his biggest headache, as he was terrified that we would not be able to seat everyone in the apparently ample space in the German School. This, then, was headache number one but we had more problems as the evening wore on. We had invited two old friends of the society. Gervase de Peyer was to perform with Gwenneth Pryor, the Australian pianist. The other performer was Norbert Brainin, the long time leader of the Amadeus String Quartet. On paper it should have worked well; in practice it was most unsatisfactory.

Gervase is a delightful person but vague on time. He asked me when they could rehearse and I told him that between four and six-thirty they could rehearse to their hearts' delight but after six-thirty I did not want the piano touched, as the tuner from Steinway turned up then to spend about one hour making sure the piano was up to concert pitch. By seven-thirty Gwenneth and Norbert had arrived but no Gervase. I was starting to get concerned as I like all my artists to be ready backstage well before the audience starts arriving. By a quarter to eight still no Gervase and I was getting desperate. At eight, still no Gervase and I was at my wits' end. What had happened? I could not get in contact with him—it was really before the arrival of mobile phones and anyway I doubt if Gervase would have had one even if they were as common as they are today. Then at about ten minutes past eight Gervase sauntered through the door and I have to say I found it difficult to keep my cool. With some rearrangement of the programme in order to let Gervase get his equilibrium we started the concert. Norbert and Gwenneth opened by playing the D minor violin sonata of Brahms in the hope this would allow Gervase sufficient time to recover. It was possibly one of the most unsatisfactory performances of the Brahms sonata I have ever heard. I admired Gwenneth's playing and it was fine in every regard but the performance did not gel in the slightest.

I suppose the rest of the programme went reasonably well but by then I was too angry to concede any satisfaction as to the quality of the performances as my critical sense had disappeared. Not a good start to the season.

Ian Hobson came to international fame when he won the Leeds International Piano Competition. His RCS recitals demonstrate a brilliant intellect and a flawless technique.

The piano recital that season—the only one in fact—was given by Ian Hobson. I have known Ian well for a number of years and he was taught by a good friend of Monica and myself, Sidney Harrison. Ian was the outright winner of the 1981 Leeds International Piano Competition. He is a man of considerable intellectual ability and is possessed of a formidable technique. His repertoire is massive and not only does he have a highly successful career as a concert pianist, but he has a growing reputation as a conductor as well as being a professor at an American university in Illinois.

Ian's approach to the keyboard is a highly intellectual one, and whilst for some it is stimulating to listen to, to others the playing might be seen as on the cool side. I can understand these two points of view. As a man, Ian is anything but cool, and he and his gifted wife Claude are delightful company. Incidentally, they have a large family of seven children. Claude is also a brilliant pianist and they appear as a two-piano duo on the odd occasion, but her appearances at the Hamilton Liszt Festival have shown what a considerable pianist she is in her own right. On the occasion of Ian's October 1995 appearance he played, for the first time at one of our concerts, the *Moonlight* sonata of Beethoven and also the two books of Paganini variations by Brahms, a test of pianistic virtuosity if ever there was one.

The Maggini String Quartet played a mixed programme at our concert in St Mary's church in Twickenham. In recent years the quartet has concentrated on rarely performed British chamber music.

Both the string quartet concerts that season were excellent. The Vellingers made a welcome return and at the end of the season we had a new quartet, known as the Maggini. They were outstanding and performed the fourth quartet by the Polish woman composer Bacewitz, which I believe won her a number of friends as a result. The Maggini Quartet have gone from strength to strength since they played for us. They hold a residency at Brunel University and have made a speciality of recording on the Naxos label rarely performed English quartets as well as the complete chamber works of Benjamin Britten.

The president's concert that season was given by an ensemble known as Opus 20, who had performed for us some seasons back. The concert shattered me in one respect. I asked Opus 20 to include in their programme the string sextet by Andrzej Panufnik and *Verklärte Nacht* by Schoenberg. They specialise in music of the 20th century and they took grasp of the programme eagerly. Little did I suspect that the mention of the name Schoenberg would strike such terror into the hearts and minds of the Richmond Concert Society. If only they had known what a romantic piece of early Schoenberg *Verklärte Nacht* is they would have wallowed in the exotic tonal colours of this music—but to put it bluntly they stayed away in rather large numbers. I was disappointed because they missed a wonderful evening of music-making. I think I would hesitate to programme a Schoenberg work again, although the audience have taken on board and enjoyed many other difficult music programmes. It is just the name Schoenberg that has such an effect and yet this man was in many respects one of the most influential figures in the first half of the 20th century.

One other concert did not go quite right, in that we had to substitute the artist. The original intention was to have a vocal recital by Susan Gritton who in 1994 had won the Kathleen Ferrier memorial prize. A few weeks before the recital I received an urgent appeal from Susan's agent asking if she could be released from her contract. I naturally wanted to know all the facts before making any decision and it turned out that Susan had been offered the part of Marcellina in a new production of Beethoven's *Fidelio* to be produced by Sir Peter Hall at the Rome Opera. I would be the last person to stand in anybody's way but to say the least I was not pleased. I knew that Susan was contracted to sing in *Orfeo* at the English National Opera about the same time and so I checked back with the opera house to establish what attitude they were taking. They had taken the view that they would, on this occasion, release her from her contract and I was therefore willing to follow suit.

As it happened Sir Peter Hall ran into serious backstage problems at the Rome Opera and the *Fidelio* production was cancelled. I am sure that Susan would have been compensated by the Italians but it must have been irksome for her to lose that engagement and the opportunity of working with Sir Peter, to lose the English National engagement and also the song recital for us. So what could we do about our concert? We had little time to find a replacement. I was keen, if at all possible, to keep the pianist as originally planned—Andrew West, a pianist whom I rank highly. I had heard that a young singer called Claire Rutter was making a big name for herself at Scottish Opera and had received rave notices for her performance as Violetta in Verdi's *La Traviata*. Indeed some critics went so far as to say that her appearance in this part was one of the most moving and well sung for years. I was able to obtain the services of Claire for the April 1996 recital. She sang a mixed programme with naturally quite a bias towards the operatic repertoire. The audience loved her. Later, and this happens with young singers, she decided to go off and have a family, but as I write she is now very much back in the limelight and making a fine career with appearances at all the major halls in the country, and she has sung her most famous role of Violetta at the English National Opera.

Chapter Six

"THEY LISTENED, DIDN'T THEY?"

As we were preparing to start the 1996-97 season of concerts a past chairman of the society died. Richard (Dick) Gandy passed away in September. His contribution to the success of the society was considerable, both as chairman and as a performing musician. He took over the post of chairman from me in 1979 and continued until 1992 when he handed over to John Ould. He then became the first vice-president and attended the concerts on a regular basis.

Born in Tasmania, Dick took a physics degree at Hobart University and in 1936 was awarded a Rhodes Scholarship to Oxford university. There he studied at Corpus Christi where he took a degree in mathematics. In the year the war started he joined the National Physical Laboratory and during the war designed aircraft. He married Veronica in 1940 and they lived all their married life in Teddington.

Dick had a very keen brain and excelled in two careers. His skill as an administrator was appreciated by all those who came into contact with him as the secretary of the Aeronautical Research Council and also of the Commonwealth Advisory Research Council. But there was no doubt where Dick's first love lay. Music dominated his very being and he was always in great demand as a singer. He appeared with Dame Joan Sutherland and Sarah Walker and sang the leading role in Berlioz's massive opera *The Trojans* under the baton of Sir Colin Davis.

As a lieder singer he showed matchless musicianship and I recall working with him on many recitals not only for the RCS but elsewhere. Over a number of years we performed most of the Britten song cycles for tenor and piano and I recall in particular the performances which we gave of the Michelangelo sonnets and the John Donne holy sonnets.

One can never know what drama lies ahead when one sets out on a new season. The 1995-96 season had had its up and downs; the following season although it had its moments of poignancy really turned out to be a very exciting one, and I think I can say that each of the nine concerts of the 1996-97 season had something to offer and cherish in one's memory. Some new music was introduced and in a number of the concerts we departed from the standard repertory. I have noticed over the years how the audience of members has changed. They tend to be more adventurous, unless there is dear old Arnold Schoenberg listed on the programme.

Although he made an impact when he won the 1981 Leeds International Piano Competition, since that time Vladimir Ovchinnikov's career has not really maintained the impetus a competition such as Leeds provides. He is a very fine and sensitive artist and it does throw into focus the problems with the music scene in this country and I am sure elsewhere. Here, with the help of a few influential promoters, a musician can be made well known over what seems a short period of time. However, there are many very fine pianists who do not have this good fortune and, to be honest, there are some well known artists who do not deserve the publicity that attracts people to their concerts. In music there is nothing fair and I could without too much effort compile a fairly long list of brilliant but unknown pianists. Sometimes the concert halls of London seem like the arenas of ancient Rome when the emperor's downward thumb denoted death.

Vladimir Ovchinnikov played an unusual programme, possibly one not designed to warm audiences towards him. He included the strange music of Scriabin, who has a greater fascination for pianists than for audiences. He also played the second sonata by Rachmaninov, not in the normally accepted form with the composer's cuts, but in the original uncut length. It is an impressive piece requiring a high level of virtuosity.

We have been helped financially over a number of years by the Hampton Fuel Allotment Charity. This is the largest charity in the Richmond upon Thames borough and the society was highly regarded by the original chairman of the trustees, Prebendary Robin Rogers. He accepted our invitation to become a patron of the society and when he died in 1996 the society wanted to do what it could to show its gratitude by organising a memorial concert. This was given by a group of advanced students from the Royal Academy of Music directed by the well known violinist Erich Gruenberg. I knew Erich as a student at the Guildhall School of Music and Drama and actually competed against him in a duo competition. We talked at some length about how we could build a suitable programme and although we had agreed that *The Four Seasons* by Vivaldi could take up all the second half we found it difficult to design an attractive first half. After much discussion we decided upon the violin concerto which Andrzej Panufnik had composed some years earlier for Yehudi Menuhin and which proved an excellent choice. As a starter we opted for the *Holberg Suite* by Grieg.

This concert was held in the main hall of Hampton School and although I had been warned that the acoustic was not of the best I was surprised how satisfactory it turned out to be, possibly any acoustic short-coming being overcome by such a strong instrumental team on the stage. This was very much Erich Gruenberg's special class at the Royal Academy and the level of talent of these young performers was quite remarkable. Erich himself took the solo part in the Panufnik concerto and the audience reaction was very positive to this piece. After the interval we all sat down to hear a performance of Vivaldi's *Four Seasons*—such a well known piece which is really four miniature violin concertos, and on this occasion the technically difficult solo part in each concerto was played by a different student.

Over forty years I recall one concert which was tinged with sadness. It was the November concert at the German School and was given by a well known ensemble called Capricorn. I did the original negotiation with the founder and leading light of the ensemble, the cellist Timothy Mason. We were able to agree on the financial side without too much difficulty and, as it happened, the programme content also got settled to our mutual satisfaction. I wanted them to play the Elgar piano quintet and Tim wanted to perform the Dvorak A major piano quintet. We settled on this programme quickly, which was a relief (it does not always happen this way). Then it is always my custom to make sure that there are no snags, so I make contact about a month before the event to see that everything is in order. On this occasion I could make no contact and I started getting slightly anxious. As the day of the concert drew near the silence remained and then a lady phoned me up and apologized for not getting in contact earlier but they had a problem at their end—Tim was not well but was determined to do the concert.

On the day of the concert the whole ensemble turned up to rehearse and clearly Tim was not at all well and after the rehearsal we had to make up a bed for him to rest on. He came on to the platform and the whole group gave an inspired reading of the Elgar quintet. Then in the interval Tim retired to rest on the made-up bed to be ready for the performance of the Dvorak piano quintet, a work of radiant well-being. The audience knew nothing of the drama going on backstage. Tim Mason had played his last concert, as a few weeks later he died of cancer. The courage he showed was extraordinary and knowing the background I found myself close to tears at the sheer guts of a musician battling against great odds to play music he loved.

In Tim's obituary in The Times soon after his early death, mention was made that during his last days in hospital many of his friends came to say goodbye and Tim could not understand how he could have touched the lives of so many, or why so many would want to come and visit him in hospital. This was so characteristic of this very modest man.

The concert was also unusual in another way. The weekend before the concert there had been a large fire on Eel Pie Island in Twickenham. It was possibly caused by a firework as it was close to Guy Fawkes night. On the island many artists lived and worked and as a result of the fire had lost everything, including equipment and work in progress. It was a major disaster and I felt that the RCS, always known for their generous spirit, would want to contribute something to help the unfortunates who had lost everything. I asked the inventor Trevor Baylis if he would make an appeal as he lived on the island. Well known for his invention of the wind-up radio, Trevor had his own inimitable style when he spoke to the members of the RCS—I am sure it was the only time they have been addressed as "boys and gals". As one could imagine, the generosity on the part of the audience was considerable and several hundred pounds were collected and passed on to the appeal office which had been set up. It took months to get the island back to some semblance of normality but many artists, having lost their means of livelihood, never actually returned to the island.

I have tried, in looking at past seasons, to dwell on particular concerts as it would be tedious for me to list each concert however good it might have been. I do have a problem with the 1996-97 season as each concert is worthy of mention but nevertheless I will still try to limit any comment to just a few more.

In January 1997 we invited the winner of the 1996 Kathleen Ferrier memorial prize, Geraldine McGreevy, to give a performance of the complete *Italian Songbook* of Hugo Wolf with the young baritone Paul Robinson. The concert attracted a capacity audience and this I felt was a breakthrough because from my earlier remarks you will have seen that lieder recitals were not at the top of the popularity stakes and the name of Hugo Wolf is not an audience-puller. Because I have lived with this kind of music for many years I find it difficult to understand why this should be. Anyway the fact that we have always insisted that our programmes must be musically balanced and include a vocal concert was beginning to be accepted, and I am sure that many members have found in the songs of Schubert, Schumann, Brahms and Hugo Wolf a whole new experience. We decided to dedicate this performance to the memory of Dick Gandy. It was the obvious concert to remember Dick by as he loved the music of Hugo Wolf and had performed the *Italian Songbook* with Hilde Beale many years before. It was a lovely performance by both artists and certainly Geraldine has gone on to achieve notable success on the musical scene.

The Muriel Dawson concert that season was given by Rafal Zambrzyscki-Payne, a very young and brilliant violinist who a few months earlier had won the BBC Young Musician of the Year competition. He gave an excellent recital and was accompanied by Carole Presland, a pianist of considerable talent whose career has blossomed since her appearance in March 1997.

Again at St Mary's church on the riverside at Twickenham we presented a string quartet concert and this time it was given by the internationally known Chilingirian Quartet. It was many years earlier, in 1969 to be exact, that the leader of the quartet, Levon Chilingirian, then a student, had led the orchestra of the Royal College of Music at a concert at the same venue. They played wonderfully well and included possibly my favourite Schubert quartet, the late one in G major. After the concert Camilla Panufnik invited the quartet, some close friends and the executive committee to her home at Riverside House and there we could relax and chat with the quartet. I recall that Levon took me aside and advised me to look very closely at a new quartet which was still studying at the Royal College of Music and which was being coached in the art of quartet playing by the Chilingirians. They were known as the Belcea Quartet and I promised that I would keep them very much in mind for a future season, and indeed this is what I did.

All I could do as musical director was try to design a series of nine concerts to form a season and to make sure that there was a reasonable balance between different types of chamber music and that the quality of artist engaged was sufficiently high. The decision as to the actual programme rests with the executive committee of the society and they have every right to suggest a change if they feel that I have weighted the society too heavily towards, say, string quartets or piano recitals.

Certainly in the past few years I have found the executive committee very strong and knowledgeable. Their expertise I have found stimulating and as a number of members of the executive attend concerts regularly, sometimes as often as three or four times a week, for no other reason than that they love music, I respect their judgment. For example, I rely on Valerie Chinchen whose knowledge on singers is first rate. She was an early admirer of Ian Bostridge and many other singers and when she gives a favourable report on a particular artist I listen. Another member of the executive is Richard Oake and his strength lies in listening to string quartets. Sometimes I think Richard spends all day listening to quartets on his hi-fi equipment and most evenings and weekends listening to them in the flesh. He is particularly interested in the contemporary scene and his views are always worth noting.

Two other members of the executive who have been on the committee for many years, Patricia Smith and her husband Ray are also regular concert-goers. Patricia joined the executive committee in 1987 and Ray joined in 1993, and very informative views come from both of them. Incidentally, Ray has made himself responsible for choosing the wine that we serve during the intervals.

With such a strong committee I wonder frequently: why the need for a musical director? As I see it, after some forty years doing the job I can perhaps have an input on the overall balance. What I do know is that the executive committee, as we reach our 40th year, consists of a collection of individuals who are all friends and it is this tie of friendship which I believe is a major factor in the success story of the RCS.

The longest serving member of the executive committee, apart from myself, is without doubt Paul Bowen. Paul also has a vast background in music, being related somewhere along the line to Schubert—I can't beat that. He has been the conductor of a Hounslow orchestra, an administrator on what was effectively the Hounslow Arts Council although they adopted quite a different name, and a critic writing for various newspapers such as the Middlesex Chronicle and the Richmond and Twickenham Times. Paul's involvement goes back to the 1986-87 season when he became the society's treasurer, succeeding Harry Curwen, a wonderful character. Paul has done this job conscientiously all these years and deserves a medal. But he has done so much more besides. It is Paul who prepares the brochure for printing every season; it is Paul who takes the floppy disc containing the programme notes for the next concert which I have written and then, through his expertise with the computer, is able to draw up a reasonable programme, given the content of what I have written. I am however still baffled as to why he gives the full name of each composer in the programme. I don't know where he gets his information from but sometimes I wonder if a named composer in the programme would recognize all his names!

The position of secretary of a society such as the Richmond Concert Society is quite a responsibility and we have had only a few secretaries over the years and each one has been outstanding. After the initial years Mary Cadman added a great deal to the society and kept everything very tidy; I have referred to her notes time and again in writing this history. Denise Latimer-Sayer followed Mary and she also had much to offer and I know what a tower of strength she was to Dick Gandy who lived just around the corner. Since 1993, when Denise retired and became a patron of the society like Mary Cadman before her, we have been fortunate in having Peter King as our secretary. Peter is someone you can rely upon to do exactly what is needed and if for one reason or another he is unable to complete the task himself then he will make sure someone is detailed to do it and this someone is generally Jo, his wife. The secretary is to a large extent the window to the world outside and it is the secretary's name which appears in various musical books of reference. In view of this he gets most of the telephone calls, brochures, and so on, from musicians all over the place who wish to perform at a Richmond Concert Society event. All this information he collects and hands over to me so that I can assess it when I come to think about the new season.

The other key person on the committee is the membership secretary. For years this job was done by Joan Stratford in a most efficient way but in more recent times, after Joan retired, the role has been taken by Jill Warner who maintains all the standards set by past membership secretaries. It is Jill who receives all the applications for membership of the society and who maintains a register of members. And it is Jill who unfortunately receives much of the flak when we get to the point of refusing new members—but she handles all this with tact and desirable firmness.

For the start of the 1997-98 season we welcomed back a quartet which had impressed everyone on their previous visit—the Vellinger—and on this

The Vellinger's performance back in 1994 of the Elgar quartet and the Janacek first quartet had remained vividly in the memory. On their second visit to the society, their playing of one of Beethoven's Rasumovsky *quartets also impressed.*

occasion they performed a Haydn quartet and a Mendelssohn quartet in the first half and one of the Beethoven *Rasumovsky* quartets after the interval.

I cannot look back at the next concert with any particular pleasure. The pianist was the great Radu Lupu and, in my opinion, his playing is quite exceptional. The problem was that the day before the recital, which I knew would attract a large audience, his manager made contact and said that there were grave doubts if Radu would play. It was difficult to get to the bottom of his problem but it seemed that he was upset that a concert that he had given on the Sunday evening went badly. He felt unwell and thought that either he had had a heart attack or he was going to have one at any moment. The day before his date with the RCS was taken up by seeing his medical consultant at an address in Harley Street. Thankfully nothing amiss was found. It was a nerve-racking experience waiting to see if he was or was not going to play for us and I tried to keep cool and collected. I was neither.

I decided, as the position seemed so worrying, to ask my old friend Martino Tirimo if he would stand by just in case Radu decided he could not, or indeed would not, perform. Martino agreed, despite the fact that he was teaching at Morley College that evening. As it happened Radu felt that he could do the concert after all and arrived at midday, not so much to try out the Steinway nine-foot concert grand we had brought into the German School but to find a suitable chair he could sit on. Piano stools are very important but Radu, because of a back problem, is unable to use a normal piano stool so has a chair instead. We had collected quite a number of chairs for him to try and eventually he found one to his satisfaction. He then sat down and did not try the instrument with any particular piece of music but just allowed his fingers to caress the keys. It was magic and I have never in my experience heard such a wonderful touch from any pianist. He only stayed about thirty minutes and then left to go home to rest.

The recital itself had moments of sheer magic once he had settled down. He started with Schumann's *Faschingsschwank aus Wien*, a work he has performed for years, and frankly I found it most disappointing. His performance of the complex Janacek sonata and the Bartok *Out of Doors* suite was quite another matter. After the interval he gave a performance of Schubert's great C minor sonata which was memorable and then, the concert over, Radu relaxed and was quite charming to all his friends who had come miles to hear him. A strange, complex man but a great artist.

That season we had three string quartets and altogether we heard three Haydn quartets which are always well worth listening to. I believe it was Eric Blom, that fine critic on The Birmingham Post when I was a boy, who once wrote, "There is no composer with whom familiarity breeds greater love and respect." Although Blom was writing about Mozart, a composer on whom he wrote a number of books, the remark could apply quite as well to Joseph Haydn.

Apart from the Vellinger Quartet we had a quartet from France, the Quatuor Parisii, who played the César Franck quartet, a long but rewarding work to hear, and which had not been programmed for some seasons. And in January we heard for the first time the young and quite brilliant Belcea

Quartet, who, you may recall, had been strongly recommended to me by Levon Chilingirian at Lady Panufnik's after-concert party at the end of the previous season.

Towards the end of the 1997-98 season we had two concerts of quite exceptional merit. Joan Rodgers is a person of immense charm and dynamic

Joan Rodgers, a wonderful singer whose ability to communicate is almost unique.

platform personality. She came with the pianist Roger Vignoles, who was returning to the RCS after an interval of many years, and together they gave possibly one of the most outstanding song recitals we have ever presented. I recall especially her performance of Mussorgsky's *Nursery Songs* sung in Russian, a language very familiar to Joan. It was this rarely heard cycle that we programmed all those years ago when Oda Slobodskaya performed it for us in the very early days of the society.

The other recital certainly deserving of mention was the return of Valerie Tryon, a pianist who has been associated with the society from its earliest years. On this occasion she played two ballades and two scherzi by Chopin in the first half and a group of Liszt in the second part of the concert. Valerie is one of the most instinctive pianists I know. She is a natural Chopin player with a most secure sense of the structure of the work she is performing. About the time of her recital CBS had released her recording of all the Chopin ballades and scherzi which had received a most enthusiastic reception by the critics including that doyen of critics in America, Harold Schoenberg. He had written of Valerie's performance that in his opinion he "would put this disc among the best Chopin recordings of the last decade". High praise indeed from a critic feared for many of the views he has expressed over the years about pianists in particular.

At the end of the season Joan Stratford, our membership secretary, retired after many years in this role. She was succeeded by Jill Warner, who was known to many members of the committee. Without any fuss or delay she got down to the vital task of sending out the brochures and membership tickets. We had started taking membership applications at the last concert of the previous season and whilst I believe this is an excellent thing to do it does on occasions present some problems for the membership secretary because membership cards and brochures are not available at that time. By the end of the season it is reasonable to say that the programme of events for the next season is almost completely in place. What may still need to be done is the booking of the venues and the approach to the sponsors of the concerts who are so vital to our survival. All this takes time, especially as we enter the holiday period and getting hold of people starts becoming difficult. Then we need to design the brochure and get it printed with the membership cards before we are in a position to get the chairman's letter and all the other items into the post.

In view of the worries we had about the Radu Lupu recital in the season which had just ended, and the standby of Martino Tirimo should Radu cancel, we all felt that we should ask Martino to give a recital to start the season off. He had intended to perform the Liszt sonata but due to a bout of flu, just before the concert he asked me if he could substitute Schumann's *Humoresque* in its place. In the circumstances I agreed and with a few hours in hand wrote a programme note on this piece for insertion in the programme. Despite feeling a bit off colour Martino played beautifully the short A major sonata of Schubert and Schumann's fantasy in C major. He is one of the most sensitive Schumann pianists I know and even when he is feeling the effects of flu is still worth hearing.

Looking back on this season I feel it worked. It possibly had a better balance than the previous season which had been dominated very much by the string quartet format. That season we had had four string quartets including the student string quartet that performed at the annual general meeting. In the 1998-99 season we had two quartets—the Janacek who made an excellent impression and the young Belcea who had clearly pleased members when they had performed in January 1998. For the second time that season we needed to make a programme alteration. I dislike doing this but every now and again we have to agree to it, although in the case of the Belcea's change I think it could have been anticipated. What happened was this. The Belceas, who are always keen on putting forward interesting programmes, had included the only quartet Delius had written, known as *Late Swallows*. I do not rank it as a particularly good piece of music, in fact it is to put it bluntly boring. With a good deal of reservation I accepted it but when the Belceas got down to rehearsing the piece they came to the same conclusion and asked if they could replace it with the *Lyric Suite* of Alban Berg. When they played the Berg piece at St Mary's church in Twickenham, a venue they regard as one of the best, they gave it an amazing performance considering that it was the first time they had performed it in public. True, there were points of detail that one could argue with but this highly talented quartet had mastered the Berg idiom, which is quite an achievement. It is not easy music but the audience listened attentively and as far as I could gather half admired it and half loathed it.

The Florestan Piano Trio came to the society for the first time as a trio although the violinist of the trio, Anthony Marwood, had played for us in an earlier season with the Raphael Ensemble. They are a fine trio and have well deserved all the acclaim they have received for their recordings which have won a number of awards. In the audience for this concert were a number of professional musicians who had come to hear them play a Haydn piano trio followed by a trio which Debussy had written in his youth but which required some reconstruction and, in the second half, Dvorak's *Dumky* trio.

We also had a new type of concert this season especially aimed at young musicians who had finished their training and were on the first rungs of a difficult musical career. This type of concert had been made possible by a generous donation given to the Richmond Concert Society from the estate of a certain Paul Woodhouse. I never knew Paul Woodhouse, and neither did anyone else in the society, but one of his executors was living in Richmond and had mentioned to the Richmond Parish Lands Charity that there was a certain amount of money available to help the arts. I met with Peter Willan, the executor, and we discussed various options. The first Paul Woodhouse concert was given by the outstanding young violinist Katherine Gowers and the pianist Charles Owen. They had just won the Parkhouse award. They performed the Janacek violin sonata and the Franck sonata. A shorter work by Messiaen was also included in the programme.

The president's concert that season was a visit by the outstanding British tenor Ian Bostridge who came with his regular accompanist, Julius Drake. This recital was clearly the highlight of the season for many and the amount of enquiries we received was greater than for any concert since the du Pré concert many years before. I received calls from our membership secretary Jill Warner saying that her telephone had never stopped ringing and that many enquiries were from non-members of the society. I had to take this seriously and I decided to prepare a contingency plan. As it happened the church was very full indeed but Jill's warnings about possible overcrowding had been heeded and in the front there were just a few unfilled seats, otherwise every seat had been taken. It was a memorable recital consisting of a few well known Schubert songs in the first half but many which were not particularly familiar. The second half consisted of Hugo Wolf songs, sung with a wonderful appreciation of the poetry, and this ability to convey a poem's meaning is one of the great strengths of Ian Bostridge's art.

And so we looked towards the end of the decade—a decade that had seen a number of major changes in the way the society operated and a period when we had established ourselves as a major arts provider in the Richmond borough with a growing reputation in the country.

In 1995 we had increased the subscription to £25 and we maintained this level until the 2000-2001 season. One change we did introduce in 1997 was to provide concerts at half the normal subscription for those on income support—a step which was certainly appreciated by those who were not able to afford the full subscription. As I have mentioned on a number of occasions we are not a profit-making organisation; we exist to provide music-making of a high standard. We are only able to provide this service because everyone who is involved with the society does so without any financial inducement. Costs do rise and certainly the cost of hiring an instrument like a nine-foot concert grand from Steinway, which has a value of just under £100,000, grows each year. In addition we have the insurance costs involved with each piano hire and of course the venue cost. But above all, bearing in mind the quality of artists we engage, piano hire must be our major outlay.

The 1999-2000 season got off to a great start with the first visit of the famous Nash Ensemble to the society. There were a number of reasons which led to their appearance in September 1999. Since we started all those years ago we had never programmed Schubert's *Trout* quintet and there was a good reason for this, as it is an expensive piece to perform as not only do

The Nash Ensemble is among the leading chamber groups in the country. The pianist Ian Brown (standing left) has performed several times for the society.

you need a piano but a double-bass as well. I am a great admirer of the double-bass player Duncan McTier and he is a regular performer, when required, with the Nash Ensemble. Duncan is also a near neighbour of mine but had never performed for the RCS although his wife, Yuko Inoue the viola player, did play in a recital with Susan Milan some years ago.

I thought that if Duncan was coming to play the *Trout* quintet he ought to have an opportunity of showing off his virtuosity in a solo item as well. Now the organisation that runs the Nash Ensemble prides itself quite rightly on the scale and ingenuity of its programmes and here was someone who did not fall in with the standard programme. I had my way and Duncan performed, to everyone's delight, a piece by Bottesini based on themes from a Bellini opera *La Sonnambula*. He brought the house down and rightly so.

All the concerts that season were of a high standard. The Gould Piano Trio were quite outstanding in their performance of the Tchaikowsky A minor trio and every time we include this work in our programme it draws more and more admirers. I was much taken by the pianist who had joined the trio, Benjamin Frith, another unsung British pianist of quite amazing ability. This concert gave me much pleasure as the Gould trio played at the first of the Muriel Dawson concerts and now here they were back with a well established reputation as a leading piano trio.

The season also welcomed back after a period of thirty years John Lill. He gave a most impressive recital, the crowning glory being the sixth piano sonata by Prokofiev. John certainly wanted to play this work but I must admit to having some reservations. It is not an easy work to hear or understand and as it is like a piece of musical granite I wondered what the audience would make of it. I need not have worried—they were carried away by the

The Gould Piano Trio, now one of the foremost piano trios in the country, came to the society when they were students and took part in the first Muriel Dawson concert.

sheer brilliance of John's performance. It was lovely having John back. He had been a patron ever since the late 1960s and is a charming man in every respect. He likes to be very quiet before a recital and we took pains to respect his wishes, but after the concert he was quite prepared to chat with anyone.

The last concert of the 1990s took place on the 14th December and was a string quartet concert by the Tippett Quartet with the brilliant young cellist Natalie Clein playing some Bloch and the second cello part in the Schubert quintet. It was a concert which had problems that arose a couple of months before the performance date. I had the founder and leader of the quartet on the telephone nearly in tears as she had fallen out with other members of the quartet. I could see both points of view and did what I could to help both sides over this crisis. The intensity of quartet playing does make them vulnerable to personality clashes and this was the case here. The leader had a passionate involvement in her quartet and demanded total commitment from all her fellow members. This was, of course, perfectly understandable but nobody expects to make a reasonable living just from playing string quartets, and, especially if you have a young family to support, you need to seek other work wherever you can get it. This nearly brought the Tippett

The Wihan, the celebrated Czech string quartet, gave a memorable concert in St Mary's church in Twickenham which is a perfect venue for quartet concerts.

Quartet to the point of collapse and this gave me some worry as the December 1999 concert was to be the occasion when Stephen Dodgson's fifth string quartet was to receive its first performance, and I did not want to let Stephen down. As it happened it all turned out satisfactorily in the end, but with another leader. They rehearsed the Dodgson quartet and it did receive its first performance, so altogether we have been responsible for the first performances of two of his piano sonatas as well as this quartet. And so the 1990s closed with the glorious sound of Schubert's string quintet ringing in our ears as we were all preparing for the new millennium.

Among the outstanding concerts of the rest of that season was the first visit of the Wihan String Quartet who some years previously had won the International London String Quartet Competition. This was the president's concert of the season and was outstanding in every respect. The vitality of this hightly talented group, who had stayed together for many years, gave immense pleasure to everyone present.

The 39th season opened on the 25th September 2000 with another visit by Valerie Tryon. Valerie has been almost the resident pianist of the RCS for much of its lifetime. A patron of the society for many years Valerie still looks young and attractive on the concert platform despite the passing of the years. As a player she seems to get better and better and her performance of the Ravel *Miroirs* was a revelation. She also played a group of Chopin including the B flat minor sonata and gave further evidence, should it be needed, that she is a superb interpreter of Chopin's music. She has been honoured many times in many countries for her contribution to music—the Hungarian Ministry of Culture have awarded her the coveted Liszt medal and in the early part of 2001 she was made an honorary doctor of music by a Canadian university.

This concert was sponsored by Kay Williams, who has been so generous to the society for a number of years. She is a delightful lady, full of enthusiasm. We were so pleased that she accepted our invitation

Kay Williams, a generous benefactress of the society for several years.

to become a patron of the society. Without people like Kay Williams and Stanley Grundy it would be impossible to run the society.

We heard in October another outstanding group of musicians known as the Fibonacci Sequence and this came about in a fairly unusual way. I had long wished to programme Ravel's exquisite introduction and allegro for harp, flute, clarinet and string quartet. It is not an obvious combination and I discussed with the Fibonacci Sequence a programme to fit around the Ravel but which made as much use as possible of the various instruments. By starting with a Mozart flute quartet and a couple of

Stanley Grundy CBE—a generous sponsor not only to the RCS but to many local organisations.

pieces for flute and harp we gave these instruments plenty to do. The clarinet took centre stage in the second half in a performance of the Brahms clarinet quintet. At first we had thought of having the Mozart clarinet quintet as the second half item, but it was decided that the Brahms piece would fit in better, as we had already decided on a Mozart flute quartet as the starting piece.

At the end of 2000 we invited back the Florestan Piano Trio and they performed a Haydn piano trio, Beethoven's *Ghost* trio and Schubert's glorious B flat major piano trio which took up all the second half. I wondered if we would get an audience for this concert. It was getting near Christmas and the weather was awful with the rain beating down. Added to this was the congestion on the roads as it was the day of the Oxford and Cambridge Varsity match. I need not have worried as St Margaret's Catholic church was full to capacity. I commented to a number of friends what a hardy audience the members of the RCS were—and rain and traffic problems were not going to deter them from a great evening of music-making! The Florestan Piano Trio go from strength to strength and their recordings of the piano trios of Schumann and Dvorak have been highly praised. A week after their recital they were going to record the Schubert work; when released some months later it was highly acclaimed.

The first concert of 2001, which marked our 40th birthday, took place in St Mary's parish church in Twickenham and was given by the Belcea Quartet making yet another appearance. They love performing in this beautiful church and their playing of the two Janacek quartets proved riveting. I gave as much background as I could in the programme about the strange relationship between Janacek and the much younger woman, Kamila, to whom he left all his worldly goods, thereby effectively cutting his long-suffering wife out of his will. The Janacek/Kamila story forms the basis of the second quartet, known as *Intimate Letters*, and the first quartet, the *Kreutzer*, is based on a short story by Tolstoy.

In February we were presenting a major concert of the season, a visit by the Guildhall Strings, an excellent ensemble of thirteen instrumentalists. This concert had been some four or five years in mind and earlier negotiations had broken down on account of repertoire. Now we had agreed upon a programme acceptable to both parties which included Britten's *Variations on a Theme of Frank Bridge* as well as some Michael Tippett and a neglected minor English composer, Armstrong Gibbs. Working with Jeremy Woods, the manager of the Guildhall Strings, we decided that the German School was an ideal venue for the concert, with its stage certainly large enough to include all the string players. Then came a hitch—well it was more than a hitch—and it created a major problem. We had been made aware that there might well be a problem using the German School for the concert, the reason being that they were going to build a new computer block in the grounds and this could prevent cars parking. It was a blow and we had to let members know that the concert would be moved to St Margaret's Catholic church. Peter Willan made a map of the church to see if there was sufficient space for the performers and there was—just. We carried out an exercise at the January concert to tell as many members as possible of the change. Those who were not at the concert we had to write to. It was quite an effort to make sure that every member knew of the venue change. The concert itself was, in my opinion, an outstanding one with a very high quality of musicianship.

The Paul Woodhouse concert was held in March and was given by the Kungsbacka Piano Trio. This highly talented group are represented by the Young Concert Artists Trust, with whom we have very close relations. At my request they prepared and performed the piano trio in G minor by

The young Kungsbacka Piano Trio played at St Margaret's Catholic church at the start of their career, and performed piano trios by Haydn, Brahms and Smetana.

Smetana and as always it worked well in the concert hall. Simon Crawford Philips, the pianist of the trio, told me afterwards how grateful the trio were to be asked to play the Smetana work and that they were going to include it in future in their repertoire. Indeed, they were due to perform it at their Carnegie Hall debut concert in 2003.

I was also much taken by Mark Stone, a young baritone who sang a concert of English songs at the April concert. He included Butterworth's *Shropshire Lad* song cycle and Gerald Finzi's *Earth and Air and Rain* cycle. What impressed the audience was Mark's very professional approach and I am sure he will have a good career.

The final concert was the most complicated we have ever mounted. Judging from the number of letters and telephone calls I received afterwards there is little doubt that it was considered to have been one of the best concerts not only of the season but for years. I am glad about this as it created a great deal of work. It all started some two years ago when I was having lunch with Ian Hobson in London. At the University of Illinois, where he is a professor of music, Ian formed a chamber orchestra a number of years ago, called the Sinfonia da Camera. It is regarded as the main chamber orchestra of the American mid-west, and its many recordings have been well received. Ian wanted to bring the orchestra to the UK and wanted my help on the practical details. It did involve a great deal of work and for months and months I was in daily e-mail contact with the orchestra's general manager, Rebecca Hill-Riley. I advised on a short three-concert tour, as the orchestra was quite unknown in the UK. I fixed up the Queen Elizabeth Hall as the first venue although I doubted they could fill the hall. I also fixed up a concert at the Fairfield Hall in Croydon and all this resulted in the third and final concert, for the Richmond Concert Society, being held on a Thursday evening, which as it happened, was Ascension Day.

To give some idea of the amount of work involved I had to make application to the immigration authorities for some thirty-eight work permits, and at one stage it looked as if the authorities would refuse entry for one reason or another. Anyway, I was able to argue my way and work permits were issued. Then I had to deal with the inland revenue foreign entertainers department on the whole question of UK earnings.

When they appeared for the RCS I thought I had everything in place but things went wrong. I had arranged for them to come over in the late afternoon from central London but I wanted their stage manager to come to the German School earlier in the afternoon to arrange the chairs and stands and in particular the large percussion section which was necessary for the Rodney Bennett marimba concerto. All this worked well but unfortunately there was a misunderstanding between the stage manager and the general manager over the van they had hired to bring the instruments over.

The key to the van was mislaid and they had to break into the van, get their instruments out and take taxis from central London to the German School. It all worked out in the end and the performance of the Rodney Bennett concerto was generally admired, as was Ian Hobson's performance of the Saint-Saëns second piano concerto.

Who would have thought forty years ago that the Richmond Concert Society would survive? Over the years there have been moments of crisis which threatened our survival but these were overcome because there was always a desire to succeed.

Maybe the last word should rest with Sherban Lupu, who is the concertmaster of the Sinfonia da Camera. He phoned me up after the last concert and said that the audience at the Richmond Concert Society were one of the most attentive he had ever played to, and clearly loved and knew their music. I would endorse this and I am very proud of the society which is, after all, the members.

The members of the Richmond Concert Society awaiting the start of a concert at the German School. Without the loyalty of the members the society could not have succeeded, so it is appropriate that the last photograph should be of them.

Coda

Over the past forty years there have been sixty-four members of the committee. There have been a few who have only made a contribution for the odd year but it is quite surprising how many have stayed for a number of years. As regards the officers of the society there have been relatively few who have occupied the position of chairman, honorary secretary, honorary treasurer or membership secretary.

I would like to acknowledge those who have given of their time and expertise to ensure that the society achieves its aims of giving pleasure to music lovers.

CHAIRMAN
Decia Griffiths 1961-1964
Edward Johnston 1964-1966
Howard Greenwood 1966-1979
Richard Gandy 1979-1992
John Ould 1992-

HONORARY DIRECTOR OF MUSIC
Howard Greenwood 1961-

HONORARY GENERAL SECRETARY
Edward Johnston 1961-1964
Marianne Duncan 1964-1967
Mary Cadman 1967-1979
Denise Latimer-Sayer 1979-1993
Peter King 1993-

HONORARY TREASURER
Edward Johnston 1961-1964
George Tyrer 1964-1967
Mark Moore 1967-1977
Harry Curwen 1977-1986
Paul Bowen 1986-2001
Tony Paton Walsh 2001-

HONORARY MEMBERSHIP SECRETARY
Patricia Hobbs 1963-1965

Louise Buchner 1965-1969
Mark Moore 1969-1977
Harry Curwen 1977-1986
Rainer Hersch 1986-1989
Joan Stratford 1989-1998
Jill Warner 1998-

HONORARY OPERA SECRETARY

Patricia Hobbs 1965-1968
Cyril Leonard 1968-1969
Kay Pope 1969-1970
Margaret Smith (née Sims) 1970-1980
Miranda Burgess 1980-1986
Eileen Beer 1986-1991

MEMBERS OF THE EXECUTIVE COMMITTEE (in alphabetical order)

	FROM	TO
Andrew Ayling	1999	2000
Leslie Baldwin	1973	1974
Brigit Barlo	1961	1962
Eileen Beer	1978	1992
Paul Bowe	1986	2001
Dora Brasher	1965	1966
Harold Britton	1973	1975
Louise Buchner	1963	1972
Miranda Burgess	1980	1986
Mary Cadman	1967	1979
Joan Caplan	1961	1968
Valerie Chinchen	1994	
Bill Cook	2000	
Gordon Cumming	1970	1973
Celia Curwen	1979	1992
Harry Curwen	1977	1986
Muriel Dawson	1971	1986
Marianne Duncan	1964	1967
Diana Dyer	1961	1967
Elwyn Evans	1966	1968
Richard Gandy	1979	1992
Malcolm Gray	1961	1962
Howard Greenwood	1961	
Decia Griffiths	1961	1964
Jill Grist	1961	1964

Sydney Harrison	1986	1993
Rainer Hersch	1986	1990
Patricia Hobbs	1961	1972
Doreen Hogarth	1967	1975
Ken Hopkins	1975	1983
Phyllis Huggett	1974	1992
Trudi Iles	1977	1978
John Inglis	1991	
Edward Johnston	1961	1967
Michael Jones	1982	1992
Mary Kennedy	1964	1990
Josephine King	1993	
Peter King	1993	
Denise Latimer-Sayer	1978	1993
Laurence Latimer-Sayer	1980	1999
Cyril Leonard	1967	1970
Bob Miller	1977	1987
Mark Moore	1967	1977
Helga Mott	1963	1967
Richard Oake	1993	
John Ould	1991	
Kay Pope	1968	1969
Bill Ritchie	1977	1980
Julie Roxburgh	1966	1967
Margaret Smith (née Sims)	1970	1980
Owen Smith	1974	1988
Patricia Smith	1987	
Ray Smith	1993	
Ralph Spicer	1994	
Joan Stratford	1988	1998
Miriam Swift	1991	1992
Foy Treloar	1970	1971
Gilbert Turner	1968	1973
George Tyrer	1964	1973
Stuart Ward	1964	1965
Jill Warner	1998	
Peggie Watson	1968	1972
Peter Willan	2000	
Diana Young	1961	1962

The Richmond Concert Society has over the past forty years put on well over 400 concerts. The number of musicians who have performed for the society is considerable. Many who performed years ago have gone on to achieve distinction and we derive satisfaction from the fact that we helped them at an early point in their career when every encouragement was needed.

The following lists give some idea of the quality of artist engaged by the society.

Many distinguished instrumentalists have played for the society. Since there have been so many, here are just a few who have performed.

Jennifer Bate (organ)
Hugh Bean (violin)
Norbert Brainin (violin)
James Campbell (clarinet)
Michael Collins (clarinet)
Eileen Croxford (cello)
Duke Dobling (flute)
Christopher Gradwell (saxophone)
Erich Gruenberg (violin)
Lionel Handy (cello)
John Harle (saxophone)
Janet Hilton (clarinet)
Daniel Hope (violin)
Nigel Kennedy (violin)

Susan Milan (flute)
Yfrah Neaman (violin)
Manoug Parikian (violin)
Paco Pena (guitar)
Michala Petri (recorder)
Gervase de Peyer (clarinet)
Keith Puddy (clarinet)
Marisa Robles (harp)
Krzysztof Smietana (violin)
Maureen Smith (violin)
George Thalben-Ball (organ)
Caryl Thomas (harp)
Bram Wiggins (trumpet)
Sioned Williams (harp)

Pianists have been the mainstay of our concerts. This list mainly relates to solo pianists but also includes a number of artists who have been accompanists or members of a group.

Anya Alexeyev
Bernard D'Ascoli
John Bingham
Malcolm Binns
Jorge Bolet
Ian Brown
Shura Cherkassky
Nigel Clayton
Caroline Clemmow
Imogen Cooper
Joseph Cooper
Barry Douglas
Michael Dussek
Fou Ts'ong

Peter Frankl
Anthony Goldstone
Sidney Harrison
Angela Hewitt
Ian Hobson
Leslie Howard
Graham Johnson
Benjamin Kaplan
Peter Katin
Freddy Kempf
Louis Kentner
Irene Kohler
Piers Lane
John Lill

Iris Loveridge
Radu Lupu
Dame Moura Lympany
George Malcolm
Malcolm Martineau
Denis Matthews
Leon McCawley
Heinz Medjimorec
Hamish Milne
Noriko Ogawa
John Ogdon
Rafael Orozco
Christina Ortiz
Vladimir Ovchinnikov

David Parkhouse
Vlado Perlemuter
Hans Petermandl
Peter Pettinger
Didier Picard
Gwenneth Pryor
Bernard Roberts
Jerome Rose
Mikhail Rudy

Phyllis Sellick
Yitkin Seow
Howard Shelley
Craig Sheppard
Cyril Smith
Yonty Solomon
Kathryn Stott
Keith Swallow
Martino Tirimo

Valerie Tryon
Tamás Vásáry
Roger Vignoles
Peter Wallfisch
Joseph Weingarten
Andrew Wilde
David Wilde
Rosemarie Wright

Events involving large numbers of performers have always proved an attraction to audiences. Over the years we have put on ensembles from piano trios to chamber orchestras and this has allowed the RCS to explore interesting and unusual repertoire. This list gives an idea of the quality of the ensembles who have provided many highly enjoyable evenings.

Bedfordshire Youth Orchestra
Beethoven Broadwood Ensemble
Budapest Piano Trio
Burnell Piano Trio
Cantanti Camerati
Capricorn
City of London Chamber Orchestra
Cohen Piano Trio
Dancing down the Ages - an evening
    of medieval music
Fibonacci Sequence
Florestan Piano Trio
Gaudier Ensemble
Gould Piano Trio
Guildhall Sinfonia
Guildhall Strings
Hausmusik
Haydn Trio of Vienna
Joyful Company of Singers
Kungsbacka Piano Trio
London Baroque Soloists

London Mozart Piano Trio
London Soloists Ensemble
Mladi Wind Ensemble
Music Group of London
Nash Ensemble of London
New London Choir
Opus 20
Partita
Philip Jones Brass Ensemble
Raphael Ensemble
Roger Norrington Ensemble
Royal Academy of Music Soloists
Scholars
Sheba Sound
Sinfonia da Camera (USA)
Tilford Ensemble
Touchwood Piano Quartet
Tunnell String Trio
Vienna Brahms Piano Trio
Zingara Piano Trio

We are very fortunate that we live at a time when many brilliant string quartets exist. Modern English quartet playing possibly dates from the great Griller Quartet. Careful tutoring at music colleges has brought forward a fruitful harvest and many leading English quartets have performed for the RCS over the past forty years. In more recent times we have widened our net and have included in our programmes a number of leading European quartets. The list gives a flavour of the quality of quartets heard at RCS concerts over the years.

Aeolian	*Endellion*	*Maggini*
Allegri	*English*	*Medici*
Amici	*Fairfield*	*Petersen*
Arriaga	*Gabrieli*	*Quatuor Parisii*
Auriol	*Guadagnini*	*Tippett*
Belcea	*Hanson*	*Vanbrugh*
Brindisi	*Janacek*	*Vellinger*
Campion	*Kodály*	*Wihan*
Chilingirian	*Kreutzer*	*Yggdrasil*
Coull	*Landolfi*	

From the very beginning the RCS has encouraged vocal recitals, and in this respect the society differs from many other concert societies. The song repertoire is immense, and composers such as Schubert, Schumann, Brahms, Wolf and in our own time Benjamin Britten have all composed some of their finest music for the voice. We are proud of the distinguished singers who have performed for the society and who have enlarged the horizons of many members.

David van Asch	*Decia Griffiths*	*Helen McKinnon*
Dame Janet Baker	*Paula Heins*	*Sybil Michelow*
Robert Bateman	*Raimund Herincx*	*Gillian Neason*
Astra Blair	*Martyn Hill*	*John Noble*
Edmund Bohan	*Eileen Hulse*	*Ian Partridge*
Juliet Booth	*Neil Jenkins*	*Geoffrey Pogson*
Ian Bostridge	*David Wilson Johnson*	*Joan Rodgers*
Catherine Bott	*Yvonne Kenny*	*Claire Rutter*
Brian Rayner Cook	*Dame Felicity Lott*	*Anna Raquel Sartre*
Sophie Daneman	*Ivan Ludlow*	*Oda Slobodskaya*
Meriel Dickinson	*Benjamin Luxon*	*Mark Stone*
Jacqueline Fugelle	*David Mattinson*	*Sarah Walker*
Richard Gandy	*Geraldine McGreevy*	*Ilse Wolf*

This book started with a glimpse into Richmond's musical past. The Richmond Concert Society has made its own special contribution to music in the Richmond borough over the past forty years and will, I am sure, continue to provide high quality concerts for the enjoyment of those to whom music means so much.